To

Thelma

Enjoy the adventure!

love
Danielle xx

# DETACHMENT

Danielle Staples

3P
PUBLISHING

Copyright © 3P Publishing
First published in 2021 in the UK

3P Publishing, C E C, London Road
Corby NN17 5EU

A catalogue number for this book is available
from the British Library

ISBN: 978-1-93740-44-3

Cover design: James Mossop and Cameron Bower
Picture references and special thanks to Stuart Ward

I'd like to dedicate this book to our parents who sacrificed so much to offer us a better future. The ones who taught us the right's and wrong's even though doing the right thing was not always favourable, but we are all learning from our mistakes which continues to help us grow. I'd like to personally thank them for guiding me along the path of discovering my roots, so we can now pass this on to our children and grandchildren....

# Contents

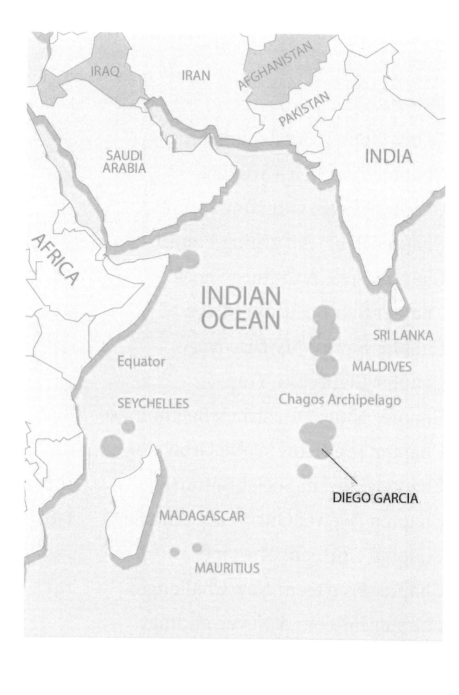

# Preface

I feel ready to share my story within this book, which is simply told as though we were sat in a coffee lounge telling you about my life, together with my deepest thoughts and feelings with revelations that may surprise some. Starting with a brief background.

Early 1960 and Mauritius is still a British colony. This small island in the Indian Ocean is a little piece of paradise, with white sandy beaches, swaying palm trees and friendly, smiling people. But with each new day that dawns, things are about to change.

London, England. Important decisions are being made in parliament to grant the island its independence. At the time, the Chagos Archipelago was administered as a dependency of Mauritius, which was keen to see the end of British rule. Sir Seewoosagur Ramgoolam was a political figure and the leader of the Mauritian Labour Party. He was to become Prime Minister once the island became self-ruled.

In 1965, part of the deal, which the British used as a bargaining chip, was to give up the Chagos Archipelago, which in turn secured Mauritius' independence from Britain. This would mean the British had full control of the Chagos Islands, and would make them part of British Indian Ocean Territory (BIOT).

Unbeknown to many, and in the process, the British formed an agreement with the USA, which paid $14 million to lease and strategically set up an army base on the largest of the Chagos Islands Diego Garcia, for air and naval defence in the Persian Gulf.

However, it would come at a cost to the inhabitants, where 2,000 or more innocent human beings would be expelled from their homeland, through trickery, fear and finally force. With no recognition of their basic rights, they were transported by boat on a one-way passage to Mauritius and Seychelles, never to be allowed to return. This act tore their nation apart, leaving its people distraught and broken in spirit, and bringing devastation. Those who docked at Port Louis in Mauritius were simply dumped and expected to find their own way. Many ended up in shanty towns, destitute, living in poverty and in squalid conditions. Some on the island resented their presence and considered them lower caste, which was not a positive start for their resettlement. Little did I know, as fate would have it, one day I would be led down a path where I'd be in a position to assist the British government in its quest to rectify the injustices suffered by the Chagossians.

During this period, there was immense opposition to the new government from many of the islanders in Mauritius. A great number of them decided to emigrate to the UK, including our extended family, while others chose different destinations around the world. The influx of new foreigners entering the UK resulted in stricter controls being placed to tighten the borders. These factors would result in our family facing a similar injustice and the beginning of our struggles.

Each member of my family can tell you his or her own incredible story, but this is my story as I remember it unfolding. I will take you along my life's journey, from early childhood to becoming an adult. I will share with you the struggles we faced as a stable family living a good life, suddenly being thrown into an ill-fated odyssey over which we had no control. Our passage proved challenging in many ways, punctuated with mysterious twists and turns, as we experienced fear and pain, with blood and tears spilt along the way.

# Chapter 1
# The Establishment

The summer of 1954.

Spending a day at the beach playing volleyball with his younger brothers and friends, Dad heard the giggles of a group of Girl Guides, who were dodging the sweeping waves, coming in and out along the shore. As he looked across, he felt a sudden attraction towards one in particular. Her permanent smile gave the impression she was a happy person, laughing and giggling away without a care in the world, and that she had a passion to care for others. (This characteristic would prove positive throughout her life.)

Dad just had to get to know her. Luckily for him, his younger brother Gerard knew who she was. His friends also became aware of his sudden interest, and together they plotted a way to attract her attention. Screaming for dear life, Dad pretended to have sprained his ankle. Naturally, she came running, and their connection was instant. It didn't take much wooing from Dad, for he ticked all the boxes; he was tall, handsome and had a certain charm about him.

After a short courtship, they were married and immediately started a family. This was typical for women in Mauritius, who were seen as primary caregivers and home-makers. Motherhood came naturally to her.

Once married, she moved in with Dad, who lived on the establishment of the sugar estate. The white colonial-style house with ten or more bedrooms came with Dad's job, located in Beau Séjour, where he worked as an overseer in the district of Rivière du Rempart. His younger brothers also followed in the footsteps of their father, who came from a middle-class family. They, too, worked as overseers on various estates around the Island.

I came along in 1957, the fourth of six children. My young life was simple and uncomplicated, detached from the goings-on outside the establishment. I can't remember reading any storybooks, but that didn't stop my inquisitive mind explore my surroundings. I'd mentally question things that baffled me. For instance, I'd see the movement of my shadow on the wall and the ground, and at times the shape would change and appear like a giant, overpowering me. I can genuinely say that it was my first ever experience of fear, although it wasn't painful. It was simply the unknown that bothered me.

Mum became aware of this. She tried to help me by explaining how we each had a guardian angel whose job was to watch over us, especially when we were afraid. She said the shadow I saw was simply my guardian angel walking alongside me, so I would never be alone and would always be protected. I'll admit, I felt reassured and my shadow became my imaginary friend.

My simple and childish way of seeing things enabled my imagination to run wild. It made my simple world more interesting and at times magical. Silly as it may sound, the stars at night led me to think that there were millions of candles alight above us because it was dark. Equally, during the day, I'd see the white clouds, which made me think that's what gave us light. Watching their formations, I'd try and make animal shapes out of them. For many years I believed they were great big balls of cotton wool that we could float on.

My fascination with ants in the garden kept me occupied for hours. I enjoyed watching the big black ones with shiny bodies bring leaves and food back and forth to their nest. It wasn't long before I found out that the red ants were the most painful. They would sting me if I disturbed their nests – served me right for not moving away quick enough! I found it amusing to see them swarm out in all directions trying to escape.

4

I loved to peel the golden sap from the bark of a particular tree and feel its texture. Of course, I just had to chew on it; it tasted of sweet caramel. However, on one occasion, I overindulged and was violently sick. Rest assured, I never opted for that delicacy again.

Seeing strangers arrive at the house was a rare thing, but I used such occasions as an opportunity to study people's behaviour: what they wore, their facial expressions and the words they used. Our native tongue was Creole, a broken French dialect, but it was more acceptable to speak French in the presence of strangers, which I thought sounded pretentious. I often found myself childishly giggling at those who didn't use or pronounce the words properly.

Our home was a pleasant and happy one, but I can't say it was ever peaceful. As kids do, we'd run around, laughing and playing outside, against the background noise of the odd cries of the younger ones, mixed with the chitchat of servants talking among themselves, the cackling of chickens and roosters' crowing. There would also be the odd bark from our family dog, Tresor, a pointer that was full of energy and very hyper. He was really Dad's dog; I can't recall playing with him at any time.

In the distance was the sound of harvesting machinery being used in the field. The estate's sugar mill provided an entirely different noise, with the clanking of steel and the hissing of steam escaping from large boilers. On a windy day, you would get the waft of a sweet smell, followed by the black smoke travelling overhead.

An old tree stood at the back of the house and a stream ran further down the field. The front had a large U-shaped drive with a garage, which my older brother Eric and sister Gert (short for Gertrude) loved to climb up and down, and on one occasion, Gert broke her arm falling from the garage top. If you knew her today, you'd question whether she'd fallen on her head instead.

Mum spent a lot of her time nursing my younger brother Jean Marc and sister Cecile. She'd be on the veranda, balancing one on her hip whilst rocking the other to sleep for an afternoon nap. The sound of her humming a soft lullaby was always comforting to hear. She had a beautiful voice, and would often sing to us. Although Mum seemed preoccupied with the younger ones, I never felt I was lacking any attention from her.

Being part of a large family had its challenges, but it was never boring. We amused and entertained ourselves and didn't see many children on the outside, apart from the servant's daughter who would sometimes join us at playtime. We'd play doll's house in the garage, then invite Mum and Dad to dinner, as it made us feel like adults. Basically, we were enacting their way of life, as they often entertained friends and Dad's colleagues on the veranda.

Dad's motorbike and Jeep came with the job. We children enjoyed riding on the back of the Jeep, and took it in turns to go for a spin around the estate. I especially looked forward to my turn. It always felt as though I got more rides, as I used to twist Dad round my little finger.

During the week, my older brother Eric and sister Marie would travel on the Tip Top Bus to school. Unfortunately, the bus didn't live up to its name, but was simply a transport company.

We weren't rich by any means, but we lived comfortably in comparison to other families in nearby villages. The palm-tree-lined private road we lived on led up to a plantation château, owned by Monsieur Lagesse. He was also the landowner and an acquaintance of Dad. The château featured beautiful colonial architecture, with a blue tiled roof. Secured by tall ornate iron railings, it proudly stood in the grounds of an immaculate landscape garden. The château appeared to have had a long history.

At times, I'd walk up to the gates and peer through the railings to absorb its natural beauty. The guards at the gate were all

6

dressed in grey military-style uniforms and looked numb. Patrolling the front gates with guard dogs on a leash, they didn't appear friendly. They were always on the lookout, and even though I tried to avoid them, they always managed to clock me and make gestures, signalling me to move away from the gates.

On one occasion, I suffered an unstoppable nosebleed and Dad was taking me to the hospital, with a towel pressed against my nose. I was holding on to his hand and trying to keep up the pace when I noticed we were walking towards the château, which confused me a little. At the same time, I was thinking we'd never get past the guards, let alone through the gates. To my surprise, the guards simply opened the gates to let us in, the same guards who watched me carefully. I was worried they might insist on us leaving, and was taken aback when they recognised me.

The housekeeper suggested that I wait on the veranda while Dad went in to speak to Monsieur Lagesse. It wasn't long before I was being led towards the deafening sound of whirling blades; a private helicopter at the back of the house was waiting to take us to a hospital.

Even though I felt privileged, the idea frightened me. Being buckled up wasn't enough to make me feel safe, because the door was still open as we lifted off and hovered a few feet from the ground. Before I knew it, we were airborne. The speed was brisk and I won't lie: the short ride was a bumpy one, which didn't help while I was trying to compress the bloody towel against my nose. I'm not sure whether I enjoyed it or not. I remember just wanting to be back on the ground.

Once in the hospital, the doctors took a close look at my dodgy nose, and the nurse used various swabs to clean up the area. Then came the needle, which looked scary. I remember crying and screaming, but for some reason I can't remember the pain of the cauterising process.

On our return, for the first time, I laid eyes on Monsieur Lagesse, who was waiting for us. A tall and well-groomed, middle-aged man, fair-skinned in appearance with greyish hair. He seemed kind. I timidly greeted and thanked him, as Dad asked me to. On leaving, we passed the guards, and one in particular gave me an assuring smile, then and every time after that.

As children we weren't allowed to walk any further than the end of our road, apart from my older brother Eric, who would at times run errands for Mum and Dad to the tabaje, our not-so-glamorous shop, which was a Chinese corner wooden shack at the bottom of the road, with a mishmash tin roof.

We had servants who cooked and cleaned, and a maid who took care of us. Dad's younger sister Janine also lived with us. She had some sort of special needs and would seem unkind at times, especially when she'd pinch our cheeks, which scared Cecile the most.

There was always a wonderful aroma drifting through from the kitchen. The servants always appeared busy cooking, washing and grinding their spices outside, sifting grains of rice and lentils in large pans.

As Catholics, we attended mass every Sunday without fail. On one occasion, whilst getting ready I accidentally peed myself, which didn't go down well with the maid. Instead of just giving me a fresh pair of pants, as punishment she made me wash and iron them dry. I was in the laundry room, which overlooked the large tree at the back of the house, feeling – excuse the pun – peed off. I was ironing, then suddenly felt an electric shock, which threw me across the corner of the room. Still in shock, I gazed out the window, where I could see a black cat sitting on a tree branch, but within seconds it transformed into a flame-haired scrawny figure all dressed in black. She was scary to look at, but disappeared just as quickly as she had appeared, leaving with an unforgettable piercing screech. I was frozen with fear. This may seem slightly exaggerated, given my wild imagination, but I'm certain of what I saw. I later found out that

Marie had had a similar experience in the same room, which convinced me even more.

Superstition on the island was rife, especially among the women. Some practised black magic. Followers of every religion formed their own spiritual beliefs, but Christians mainly shared stories of the supernatural, mixed with its curses, and old wives' tales. Mum was no different; she had similar views. After I told her about my experience, she explained that it was a sign from the spirits warning of a death in the family.

She had an explanation for almost anything uncanny, or an accident. For example, if a piece of cutlery accidentally fell on the floor, you'd hear her say, 'We're expecting visitors,' but if it was a sharp knife, then it would be, 'Someone's coming to give us bad news!' At times, we'd hear her say, 'Moffin ça!' (That's bad luck!)

There were days we'd be encouraged to crouch under the table and call out names of family members, willing them to come and visit. Strangely enough, many times this proved successful, which led me to take a similar view on the unexplained.

I don't remember my grandparents. Mum's family had already emigrated to the UK and although Dad's father was still living on the island, he remarried after the death of his first wife, which caused a rift with his family, and the reason for his absence.

In the summer months, the establishment gave us access to a beach villa, where we'd spend a few days socialising with other relatives. Although it was fun, we took it for granted. Now I'd give anything to be back there.

A typical Sunday for us was to travel crammed in two or three cars, sometimes an open-top Jeep, and spend a day in Mont Choisy. This was a popular spot for many of the locals. It had white sand that stretched for miles, and the turquoise sea was so inviting that once we got there all we wanted to do was to jump in.

Mum would opt for a shaded area and set up our picnic under a filao tree. The party atmosphere would begin once my uncle's

9

transistor radio was turned on, with traditional sega music blaring. A picnic for Mauritians meant eating, drinking, dancing and playing on the beach, then, finally, a swim before heading back home.

Dad's favourite pastime was deer hunting, with his dog Tresor and close friends. They'd travel in a classic white Volkswagen Beetle, armed with rifles. He was a sharpshooter and received many trophies at their local club in Mon Loisir to celebrate their achievements.

On Saturdays, he and his friends would go to the Champs de Mars race tracks in the capital. Combined with drinking rum and hunting, these three passions were their entertainment. The same goes for most men living on the island today.

The Maiden was an important event with horse racing fans, similar to Ascot in the UK. I clearly remember it was a family tradition to make a day of it, with everyone in their Sunday best. For me, that meant getting into my favourite blue floral dress and black patent buckle shoes, only ever worn on special occasions. Dad's turf club membership gave us a good position on the balcony from where we could watch the race. It was an exciting day out for us, as it meant we also got to meet up with other members of our extended family.

Dad was a proud man. He'd always stand with his head held up high, and he had a certain presence. His facial expression could be mistaken for strictness and that he was 'above himself'; and having said that, at times he would demonstrate his position and use a certain tone of voice when dealing with the labourers in the sugar cane fields. In reality, though, he had a kind heart and was respected by all who knew him, including his friends and work colleagues.

I, too, admired him and looked up to him. I'd often catch myself watching his ways: how he would continually comb his hair, before placing the small comb in the top pocket of his shirt. To work, he would wear khaki Bermuda shorts with a matching loose shirt, heavy woollen knee-length socks, and for protection from the midday sun a sort of pith helmet. His attire would portray a person in charge.

The island enjoys a subtropical climate, but it doesn't always come without its challenges. Storms and cyclones are very common in Mauritius due to its geographical location in the tropics. These horrendous weather conditions would occur mainly in the summer months, and have been known to destroy livelihoods and devastate many parts of the island.

Those people with homes made of straw stood no chance; those with tin roofs would see them fly off as easily as lifting the lid off a box. There was constant flooding and blackouts, leaving families with no electricity for days or even weeks. In conditions like these, children were expected to stay indoors or get thrown about like rag dolls if they got caught in them.

One of the worst cyclones the island ever witnessed was called Carol, in 1960. Mum was expected to give birth in March, but went into early labour. The hospital was overwhelmed with injured patients as a result, and the lack of care and facilities may have contributed towards Mum losing the child at birth. It was a girl. As you can imagine, everyone was devastated at this loss.

Dad was a strong swimmer. Typically, he'd take along old car tyres for us to use as floats and play in, and we'd hold on to these if we wanted to join him further out to sea. One Sunday, when I was six, we were on a family picnic on the beach. I couldn't swim that well, and recall I was positioned inside the tyre, which was secured with a rope tied to Dad's body. I held on as he swam further out, but soon lost my grip and fell through.

I didn't have time to breathe in and hold my breath. Saltwater went into my eyes. As I sank deeper and deeper, I panicked and struggled to come back up. However, for some unknown reason, as I was drowning I felt a certain calm. It was silent and in the distance, but I could make out a figure. She was beautiful, with long, never-ending hair and legs that shimmered in the water.

She was willing me to come towards her, but within seconds Dad lifted me out of the water and swam me back to shore.

Safely back on the beach, I was vomiting and shaking with fear. Even though the experience was strange, I felt compelled to go back and admire this vision, but I was being given a telling off for not holding on like I was told to.

Our day at the beach was cut short. As the car was pulling off, still in tears I looked back at the sea in the hope that I could get a glimpse of her again. A certain sadness grew in my heart and it felt as though my favourite toy had been stolen from me. It wasn't until a few years later, whilst reading a children's storybook that had pictures of a mermaid, that I was able to identify it as similar to what I saw in the water back then.

To this day I have nightmares about drowning, but the vision that came with it gives me a sense of calm. I still can't explain it, because I should have died right there and then. I told Mum about my experience, and she said she believed it wasn't my time to die. I thought about what Mum had said, and in my mind I questioned what dying meant, because if that was death then the experience is beautiful and painless.

# Chapter 2
# The Crossing

June to December is harvest time on the estate, and a busy one for labourers working in the sugar cane fields. Equipped with their serpe (sickle), they'd chop away at the base of the canes before loading them onto carts, usually drawn by oxen or cattle, and sometimes loaded on Bedford trucks, to be carried from the field to the mill for processing.

We all looked forward to Dad bringing raw canes for us to eat. We'd use our teeth to rip into the husks, before sucking on the juice to its bare fibres. The servants would make a tasty refreshing drink from molasses of golden-brown sugar cane syrup and tamarind juice with water. At the end of harvest, in celebration of their hard work, workers and managers would always reap the benefits and enjoy a drink of rum; for some reason, the Green Island brand comes to mind.

Our family was continually growing. Between 1961 and 1966, Mum gave birth to Mireille, François, Popol (our nickname for Paul), Bernard, and Shirley, making eleven of us in total. Mum and Dad had always planned to emigrate to the UK to be close to her family, but this was constantly being put on hold. I guess they were too busy popping out kids. However, in August 1966, they decided to send my brother Eric to live with our grandmother in London, where she would see him through school, allowing him an education and giving him better prospects for the future.

Unfortunately, Mum suffered some complications after giving birth to Shirley and stayed in hospital for several weeks. Eric's departure was due, so he had to say goodbye to her in hospital. I was present at the time and will never forget his distress before leaving. Naturally, he didn't want to go, as he was very close to Mum.

He grabbed hold of the bedstead, and didn't let go, begging to stay, whilst screaming and asking, 'Why? Why? What did I do wrong? I'll be good. What did I do wrong? I don't want to go.'

Seeing Eric's distress brought tears to my eyes. I felt helpless, and didn't know what to do or how to comfort him. It was a sad moment for us all. I questioned myself: *Could it be that he, too, had done something wrong? Was he being punished?* Unsure and confused about his reaction, I remembered the sadness I also felt back on the beach, for failing to hold on to the tyre.

Eric finally left for the airport with Dad. Someone had given him a bar of chocolate in an attempt to distract him. For a while, it wasn't clear as to why he had to leave and what had happened to him, but I felt a void inside me after then, which wasn't very pleasant.

Not so long after his departure, tension on the island was brewing, because the General Election was approaching independence. The country witnessed riots between the Creoles, Muslims and the Chinese, initially in the capital, but eventually, these would erupt in smaller villages around the island.

Dad had built a certain rapport with Indian labourers in the field and at times interacted with them socially, sharing a drink and cracking a few jokes amongst themselves. He even learned their lingo, which he often used in their company. This type of interaction went against the strict rules on the plantation, which caused disagreements and conflicts between him and his superiors. As an overseer, complete obedience was expected. He had to abide by all plantation regulations or else face dismissal for insubordination. Complicating this relationship was also a matter of class distinction, creating a division between the workers from their superiors to show who's boss. The prejudice of race, religion and class was to become the main issue behind the civil unrest on the island.

Towards the end of October 1966, Dad seemed more and more preoccupied at work. In the evenings, there were more work colleague gatherings than usual on the veranda, but instead of the usual laughter and cracking of jokes, their debates seemed more serious and at times heated. We were constantly being told to stay indoors, due to rioting in the streets. In nearby villages, there were many threats of kidnapping made against the sugar plantation managers and their families.

Troublemakers would often deliberately set fire to the sugar cane fields, especially before the harvest, to cause further disruptions. You could see these in the distance and smell the sweet flames, which would travel across the vast sugar cane fields, but were also frightening, as they could potentially spread to nearby properties, especially if the wind was blowing the wrong way.

My ninth birthday was approaching. I remember the family organising a party for myself, Gert and Cecile, as we were all born in the same month. We were all excited about the upcoming celebrations, but saw less and less of Dad during this time.

I remember two things about this day in particular. Although it wasn't my turn to ride in the Jeep, I had the strangest feeling that my approach to Dad wasn't going to go well, but I ignored my instincts, and ran out in haste to catch up with him as he was leaving for work. All excited, I asked if I could go for a ride around the estate. He initially ignored me, but I repeatedly begged.

Suddenly, he turned around and said sternly, 'Rentrez!' (Go inside!)

I was taken aback and confused, as he had never spoken to me in that manner unless I had done something wrong. I felt sad and rejected. That very day, Dad came home earlier than usual in a state of panic. It soon became clear he'd had a disagreement with one of his superiors. In a fit of rage, he'd told them to stuff their job, before leaving the site. He destroyed his office and attempted to set fire to the motorbike parked outside the main building.

Subsequently and without notice, we found ourselves leaving the estate. Everything happened so quickly. There was no time to think or plan; before we knew it, we were travelling in two cars heading towards the capital. We arrived at Mum's Aunt Maraine's place. They were expecting us and welcomed us with open arms.

Maraine was a kind lady. Both she and her husband Tonton André were retired. They had five grown-up children and lived in a large bungalow with an annexed extension out back. We stayed with them for a few days, before being told that Mum and Dad were sailing to the UK, but without us!

I was confused, with a familiar sadness that grew inside me. My gut instinct was telling me something wasn't right, but as children we didn't question it. As they were talking to us, I had a déjà vu moment and recognise the words being used; even the room seemed familiar. It was a strange feeling, as though I had lived it in a different life.

The day came for Mum and Dad to sail away. Marie, Gert and I accompanied them to the port in a black Morris Minor. On arrival, the area we were walking towards seemed huge. There were people everywhere, some queueing and others already walking up a sloped ramp to get on the ship. It was gigantic and I can still remember the name written on the side: *Ferdinand de Lesseps*. I remember the noise around us, too.

There wasn't much time to spend with them, and we quickly had to say goodbye. I couldn't stop crying, remembering how Eric must have felt when he left. Like him, I cried and begged to go with them, but both Mum and Dad gave us some reassuring words, that it wouldn't be long before we would all be reunited, and we were to be strong and proud, with no tears, as it showed weakness.

I felt embarrassed for crying and tried to hold back the tears, so Dad would be proud of me. I don't remember any long-lasting hugs and kisses from either of them, which wasn't unusual, because whilst growing up it wasn't an affection ever expressed by either of them. Their departure was traumatic and deeply scarred me, but I knew I had to protect myself from feeling vulnerable. Like Dad, I had a certain pride within me, and wouldn't always demonstrate how I was feeling. I tried to put on a brave face, even though deep inside I was hurting. Before the ship even departed, we were quickly scuttled back into the car and made our way back to Maraine's place.

This was probably a turning point in my life that defined the way I would form future relationships.

Leaving ten children behind must have been traumatic for them, especially Mum, because at the time the youngest was only four months old, even though in their minds they felt we would soon be reunited, once they had settled in the UK. To this day, I believe that if they had not departed on that day, they might still be in Mauritius. However, although, their decision to leave us behind seemed a harsh one, it was more a sacrifice, to offer us a better future.

Their crossing took just over a month. Their plan was to travel via Marseille, then on to Liège in Belgium, before entering the UK. During the trip, Mum became unwell. She was still recovering from a recent illness, and to top it all she had developed a terrible rash all over her body, irritated by scratching. This was probably a consequence of all the stress she was under, not to mention having to leave her children behind.

On arrival in Liège, they made contact with Dad's cousin, who suggested they stayed for a while; but their focus was to get to London to see Eric and start reuniting the family. They were not aware that Immigration in the UK had tightened the borders, which created an obstacle. Their lack of the English language proved yet another barrier for them to overcome.

Mum's younger brother Corneille travelled from London to meet them in Liège. Seeing his sister's distress and deteriorating health condition, he accompanied them to England. On arrival at customs, the officer stamped Dad's passport with a six-month permit on his visa. However, in the confusion during questioning, he failed to stamp Mum's passport. With no limitations on her papers, she was, on the face of it, free to remain.

Once Mum saw Eric and her family, she felt safer and was eager to build a home for the family. However, with the limitations on Dad's visa, this would not be easy. They stayed at my grandmother's place, which was already overcrowded.

Undocumented, Dad returned to Liège six months later, where he was happy to take on any type of work, as his savings weren't going to last much longer. He was also sending money back home for our care, as well as giving Mum enough to live on. Knowing Dad's pride, I can't imagine how it must have felt, to take on a job in a hotel as a washer-upper. No doubt, it would have dented his pride, but it showed how focused he was on seeing his family reunited, even though he knew in reality it meant being back in the UK, which wasn't going to be easy. In the coming months, he made a few attempts to re-enter the UK, but only for a short while and was always unable to remain.

Apart from being a housewife, Mum never needed to work, but she knew she had to do her bit. She found a job at a local bakery, initially as a general help. She later learned how to bake and decorate cakes, which was to become her love and passion in life.

We arrived back at Maraine's from the port. It was strange walking through this time. I was able to take in all the details of my new surroundings from the street: the large green corrugated metal door that led to a long narrow path, lined with a few palm trees, which continued into a large orchard. Beyond this was the house. Seeing the fruit trees got me all excited. I couldn't wait to be let loose to indulge in these, which included some of my favourites like masson (jujube), longan (dragon eye fruit), bilimbi (averrhoa), carambole (starfruit), goyave (guava), mango and lychees.

Their youngest daughter was Monique, and she showed us around. There were many religious statues dotted around the place and pictures of Jesus and various saints on the walls. We were shown our new sleeping arrangements. We had to share two rooms divided by curtains, but because we thought at the time that this was going to be temporary, it didn't seem so bad.

I wasn't keen on the toilet situation, as it was a small hut outside the main house – and it stank! To use it, you'd have to crouch down onto a hole dug in the ground, with old sheets of newspaper to wipe yourself with. None of us liked this facility, but we had no choice. We were given pots to use at night.

During this time, I made the most of the fruit trees and ate them until I was full to the brim. I spent a lot of my time in the orchard, where, I often had déjà vu moments. The place seemed familiar somehow, but I can't ever remember having even visited it, which seemed even more sinister.

All Maraine's children worked during the day, apart from Stella, who helped with the housework and looking after us. Mealtimes were always a challenge. A system was set up. We'd all sit in line, and someone would feed us from a large plate of food, using the same spoon. Breakfast was usually boiled rice, fried eggs and bouillon cresson (watercress soup). This was a normal diet for them. The routine was always the same, but if you didn't chew your food quick enough, you'd miss a turn. I don't know about the others, but I quickly got wise to this and would gulp my food down, not properly chewed, so I didn't miss a turn.

My first ever haircut happened whilst living there and I didn't know what to expect. Most of us were made to sit down and given a bowl cut: literally with a bowl over our heads, and simply cut in that shape! I could have cried when I saw my locks being thrown to the ground, I ended up looking like, what I can now, only describe as a *Dumb and Dumber* haircut.

When they were not praying, the house would always be filled with music and laughter. Maraine loved to play the piano and Monique taught us lyrics to French songs. She was a big fan of Cliff Richard and C Jerome, I learned one of his songs by heart. It was called 'Le Petit Chaperon Rouge Est Mort'. Marie and I would sing duets to various songs like 'Tous les garçons et les filles', a song by a popular sixties French singer named Françoise Hardy.

With not much else to do, we'd spend hours having singing competitions between ourselves. At weekends we watched *Top of the Pops* on TV. It was rare to have a TV in those days, and the neighbouring children would sit on the adjourning wall to try and get a glimpse of what we were watching.

Stella had a boyfriend named Sylvio, but who was commonly known as Fanfan. They seemed very much in love. He was tall, handsome and kind. He did, however, enjoy a drink or two, which at times fuelled their arguments. This would cause a lot of upsets and tears for Stella and there were many break-ups, but they always managed to get back together.

He truly loved and worshipped her. Watching their bitter-sweet relationship fascinated me. I studied their body language and the goings-on, and was intrigued by it all. I often found myself spying on them from behind the settee, to understand their behaviour better, especially when they'd kiss and cuddle whilst on the sofa. It was captivating, because I had never experienced these emotions before. It was like watching a secretive romantic movie.

Stella's family weren't too keen on Fanfan, mainly because of his temper and drinking habit. Although she knew this, she loved him too much to end it. When he wasn't around, I had many conversations with her about how she felt. Despite his drinking, I thought Fanfan was a lovely man. Some weekends, he and Stella would take us to a social hub called Juke Box, where young teenagers would hang out. It was a casual, open-roof bar in the capital. We were given coins to use in the machines that played the latest French songs, and this is where my love of French music came about.

Watching the dancers on *Top of the Pops* made me want to become a dancer. The girls were beautiful and looked like the models in fashion magazines that Monique would have lying around the place. Although this may seem shallow, at the time it influenced me a great deal. I often had dreams of becoming one of those girls. Watching the love between Fanfan and Stella also made me dream that one day I, too, would be loved and admired that way.

As usual, we went to church on Sundays. Me and the others looked forward to the treats after mass. The street vendors outside would sell some of my favourite cakes, like Gateaux Napolitaines. These vendors would have small metal containers loaded on the back of their bikes selling freshly made sweet and savoury snacks.

Even though Tonton André looked weak and walked with a stick, he was one of the strongest men I'd ever come across. His strength and energy were unbelievable. After mass, he'd walk us up the rugged hill to an old fortress famously known as citadel; this was his weekly exercise.

We'd only been there for a short time when news came in. Mum and Dad were facing difficulties with their settlement, and it appeared that our reunion wasn't going to be straightforward. On learning this, Maraine and other family members went about finding a solution for our long-term care. Although they loved having us, the numbers made it impossible for a longer period. They sought advice from the church, who agreed to accept us into Catholic convents, under the pretext that we had been abandoned by our parents. This wasn't true, of course. The delay in our reunion would be due to the difficulties faced at Immigration in the UK.

# Chapter 3
# Our New Family

Morning came. I woke with butterflies in my stomach, feeling nervous about meeting our new family and saying goodbye to those I'd grown close to. Life, however, has a dark sense of humour. None of us was laughing when we had to say goodbye to our brothers, not knowing when we'd meet again. Shirley was asleep when we posed for what would be the last photo taken as a family in Mauritius.

Looking around at what we were leaving behind, you could say I was glad to see the back of the latrine facilities. Once again, I had that churning feeling in the pit of my stomach, which seemed to come along when I felt I'd done something wrong or had to face the unknown. Although I felt tearful, I tried not to show this emotion, as it made it worse and I thought it might encourage the others to do the same. I held back the tears and swallowed my pride. Needing to control my feelings and make-believe this situation didn't affect me, it helped to remember Dad's words, to: 'hold one's head up in pride'.

We were divided. Jean Marc and François, were the only ones taken to the boys' convent; Popol and Bernard stayed with another relative, as they were too young to be accommodated at the establishment.

Accompanied by Stella, myself, Marie and Gert, walked to the girls' convent, Couvent Notre-Dame De Bon-Secours on Edith Cavell Street in the capital, Port Louis. Monique accompanied Mireille and Shirley who had already travelled ahead of us by car. On arrival, Stella rang the bell, and as we waited I carefully studied the outside. The grey stone wall that surrounded the convent made it look private and isolated.

There was a squeaking sound as the metal door opened. A nun peered out and signalled us to enter, as though we were expected. Inside the courtyard, two other nuns stood alongside each other, hands concealed under the tunic of their habits. They smiled, nodding their heads in an attempt to welcome us. We were briefly introduced to them as Mère Supérieure Seraphine (who was the Mother Superior), Sister Benedictine and Sister Du Calvert, who seemed kind. She wore a permanent smile on her face. We were then told to say our goodbyes. Although both Stella and Monique reassured us that they would come and visit, I still felt a certain sadness. One thing was clear, I hated goodbyes.

Then the nuns walked with us across the courtyard towards the chapel, which appeared peaceful. I watched them in awe, trying to study their behaviour, the way they walked, as though floating on air. They were all similarly dressed in immaculate long tunics over their off-white habits, they wore a veil, coifs and wimples (a close-fitting cap covering their heads and cheeks, which helps keep their headdress in place), a heavy belt made of rope around their waist and a large wooden cross with a rosary hanging from it. They also wore brown sandals. I remember thinking, *they must really feel the heat and it must take them a long time to dress themselves.*

Mère Supérieure Seraphine pointed towards an outbuilding in the distance but within the grounds, and in a harsh tone she said, 'That's the crèche where your sisters are.'

Although I knew I might not see them for a while, it gave me a sense of reassurance that we were close by.

The odd gardeners working in the grounds watched us curiously as we approached the main buildings. Even though I couldn't see them, you could hear the distant laughter of children playing. The nuns led us through an iron doorway, revealing a highly polished red floor into the corridor, with echoing footsteps and a shuffling of robes. We saw one or two nuns walking with their heads bowed down, as if eye contact was a no-no. We were told that running in the corridors was not allowed. We reached the large dinner hall, which was empty, with benches and long wooden tables already set up for the next meal.

We were then left alone with Sister Benedictine, who was very matter of fact and hardly smiled. Upstairs, she showed us the dormitory. Marie would be placed on a floor above us, because she was older. The nuns slept in a cubicle within the dormitories.

Then we were shown where we would sleep. Sets of clothing were neatly laid out on our individual beds: a pastel blue check dress, a small white hat, long white cotton nightdress, a comb, a toothbrush and a sample size toothpaste. Strict instructions were given on how to care for these or face punishment. Then we were informed our uniforms would be provided when we started school.

Daily mass was at 6am, which meant getting up at 5.30am every day. I remember thinking, *I'll never wake up at that time.* The strict regime instantly gave me the jitters.

Still with Sister Benedictine, our tour continued to the recreation ground, where there were many children, some in small groups giggling, and chatting among themselves; but this abruptly stopped at the sight of a nun as they strove to appear well behaved. They watched us as we walked by.

Sister Benedictine pointed at a small blue metal gate in the courtyard and informed us that it was the entrance to our school, which was connected to the convent. The sound of children playing and bells ringing to call them in could be heard.

I had mixed emotions about my new environment. On the one hand I felt excited to mix with other children, but on the other I had reservations about the nuns, who came across as unfriendly and regimented. Seeing a nun close up gave me the opportunity to study them even closer. Their behaviour fascinated me, so naturally I was curious to see if they were as normal as us. Their regimented ways reflected on how they ate, the way they walked and prayed. Initially, I tried to try to get a glimpse of what they looked like underneath their veil as they were getting ready for bed, but being caught meant punishment, so I quickly gave up on that idea.

At night, the lights would go out at around 8pm. Each of us was given daily chores and we took it in turns to polish the red-tiled flooring, using a dried coconut cut in half, placed under the arch of our feet or by hand. We called it brosse coco. When it was my turn, I used to dance around on these to make it more fun. Amazingly, the use of dried coconut always guaranteed a shiny floor. Some of the other jobs included working in the chapel or the crèche, gardening and various duties in the kitchen.

I began wetting the bed when I was still at Maraine's place. I'm sure some of my siblings had a similar problem, although I didn't know it for sure. The wee stench gave it away in the bedrooms. None of us let on for fear of being told off. This bad habit continued and I soon became a target for special attention by the nuns.

One morning, Gert told us about a figure, maybe a ghost of some sort, standing at the bottom of her bed in the night, which scared me and didn't help with the bed-wetting problem. I would sleep with the blanket over my face and would hold the urge to use the pot under my bed.

Some in the orphanage, myself included, experienced the harsh punishment for this terrible habit. The nuns never showed us any mercy. Our punishment was first to strip our beds and be humiliated in front of the others to set an example on what to expect for this type of behaviour. A rotin (cane) was used for the daily caning on the palm of your hands, backside or whichever took their fancy at the time. The harshest punishment we ever suffered was being made to kneel on rock salt or grains of rice holding a brick over our head, with the midday sun beating down on us for all to see. This would last an hour or so, or until our knees bled.

Initially I tried not to cry or show any emotion for the harsh treatments I received, but this only prolonged the caning or other punishment being handed down. The nuns liked to see you cry, so that's what I did a lot of the time. At night I would rock myself to fall asleep quicker to avoid facing any further discipline.

We had only been there a few days when my sisters and I found ourselves itching from top to bottom, resulting in large sores all over our bodies. Our heads were also covered in lice. Once the nuns realised what was happening, they got us together and marched us through the courtyard and down a steep stairway, which led into another small yard known as le basse-cour (the basement yard).

We were led into a dark chamber with only a bench to sit on. There was old dripping candle wax on the walls. We were stripped bare and the nuns started to smother our bodies from head to toe with a white liquid that stank of strong paraffin. We were then given long white robes to wear, with mittens, so as not to scratch. It was pure agony.

There were other rooms close by with other children suffering a similar thing. You could hear them muttering away, some crying in pain, which was scary at times. We were to remain there until the rash – which they called la gale (similar to scabies) – cleared. During the day, above us I could hear the laughter of children playing in the school playground. I just wanted to escape and run to the noise the children were making. I cried a lot during this time. It seemed as though we were there for weeks, but in reality it was only three or four days before we were allowed to go back into the main building. I knew I would never want to see that place again, and thank God I never did. However, although I wouldn't wish that on anyone, it was comforting to have had my sisters with me during that time.

Our eyes and skin colour were lighter than most and we spoke good French, which we used a lot when we first arrived. Because we were amongst strangers, this must have made us appear different from the other orphans, plus we had living parents. The nuns told us that we should be more like the others and only speak Creole, so that we wouldn't think we were anything special. Little did I know that the use of this dialect would one day prove beneficial to me.

There was one other girl who looked similar to us and her name was Ileen. She looked foreign, with beautiful long red hair and very fair features. Her time was mostly spent looking after the children in the crèche. Some of the girls with long hair would have theirs cut short, so as not to bring attention to being pretty.

My first day entering the school playground felt strange, as I had never experienced it before. At nine, I couldn't read or write. I was excited when I saw my Aunt Denise, Mum's sister, who taught English at the school; but as I skipped towards her, she seemed distant, as though she had never seen me before. She told me that she couldn't show us any preference whilst at school. Her children studied at the same school and they didn't mix with us either.

Others would tease us for being orphans. They'd call us names like milat (mulatto), and they teased me with the name lezo zozo (bird bones – bony bird, if you like). I had a complex about my skinny legs. They were the one feature I disliked about my body. (They were skinny though!)

Monsieur Douce was my French teacher. He was kind, and helped me settle in. I paid special attention in his class and found the lessons easy to understand where others struggled. Over time, I learned to read and write, and everybody in French class wanted to be my friend because I was able to help them.

After a while, my confidence grew. I made a lot more friends both at school and at the convent. My best friend's name was Ursulle. She was of similar age to me, typically Mauritian, with dark features and the widest white smile, which always made her appear happy. She always wore white tights instead of socks, because she wanted to have white legs. She went everywhere with her doll; they were inseparable.

I learnt about her reason for being an orphan. She had survived a house fire in which she lost both her parents. With no other family to care for her, she arrived at the convent at the age of five. Growing up there taught her all she needed to know about everybody and everything. We played together, and I naturally mixed with all the friends she had made, which helped make my stay more pleasant.

Ileen would occasionally give me news of Mireille and Shirley. At times she allowed me to join her when she went across to look after them, and it was nice to see them all grown up. Shirley didn't recognise me. Mireille, on the other hand, was cheeky and would giggle at anything you told her.

I was given the job of making the wafer host for mass and I helped in the offices above the chapel. Once I got the hang of what to do, I enjoyed it, because I got to eat some of the dregs. I simply had to mix flour and water in a large bowl, before spreading the batter over a hot griddle to form a large, flat, square wafer. I'd then transfer this on to a similar cutting plate to make little round hosts.

Working in the chapel included other duties that I didn't enjoy. For instance, after the death of a nun or priest, the climate being what it is, their burial was normally carried out the next day. However, until then, their bodies would be laid in the chapel overnight. Our duties were to take it in turns to sit alone in vigil, watch over the dead and recite the rosary with other sets of prayers for an hour or so at a time. This always scared me and gave me nightmares, for fear the body would come alive. It soon became clear why the others didn't like working in the chapel.

Marie and I always sang in the choir, which we enjoyed. Our love of singing eased our pain and entertained others, singing

French songs that we learnt whilst staying at Maraine's. I truly believe it helped us overcome some of our most difficult moments during our time in the convent.

Christmas was always a busy time, but fun. The choir would practise for hours in the chapel. Some of us spent time making paper chains and used colourful tissue paper to make honeycomb baubles as decorations to hang in the dining hall. Come Christmas morning, we'd expect the same gifts every year. Although we were grateful, I can't say they were very exciting. At the bottom of the bed, where a nun would have quietly placed it in the middle of the night, was a toothbrush that had to last you a year, a comb and an orange. The more underprivileged were given dolls and smaller toys donated by various charities.

Ursulle was always given a doll. She was obsessed with them and never wanted to share any of them with me, so at times we'd fight over them. You'd often find her lining them up and speaking to them; they were family to her. You would see similar behaviour with other orphans. One in particular was Matunga. Her job was to shine the children's shoes, then line them up ready to be picked up individually, many times. You'd catch her kneeling in front of them, holding a full-blown conversation with them. It did make me giggle, because I thought it was odd.

February 1968. Stella and Fanfan were due to get married and four of us sisters were to be bridesmaids. We were all excited, because we didn't get to leave the convent that often. Marie had been given hair rollers in preparation and one of the girls in her dormitory had asked her to put some in her hair. Marie agreed, but got into trouble for doing so. Shortly afterwards the girl insisted that Marie should try again, but she was caught a second time. As punishment, she wasn't allowed to go to the wedding. I recall when the three of us were leaving to go to Maraine's to get ready, Marie was sat at the top of the stairs crying her eyes out. I wanted to rush and take her with us, but I felt helpless and sad because I couldn't do anything.

The wedding was held at the cathedral, L'Église Immaculée Conception, in the capital. I was very nervous, as I had never been a bridesmaid before, but you could say I loved the attention and the pretty dress I got to wear. After the ceremony we were taken straight back to the convent, which was an anti-climax to the whole day. It didn't seem fair, but we didn't have a choice.

12th March 1968 was Independence Day on the Island, and a special celebration ceremony was being held at Champs de Mars racing ground. A few of the older girls were allowed to attend, but unfortunately I was not one of the lucky ones. We were told, though, that we would visit a British warship docked at the port. I remember being really excited. I thought it would give me a glimpse of what Mum and Dad had experienced when they left the island.

The day came, and sure enough, ten of us went on this trip with two nuns. The area looked the same as I remembered it, but the ship was different. It was painted grey and looked very mechanical. It was very noisy. There were many people standing around admiring the ship, some taking photographs.

We followed sister Benedictine up the slope, and at the top was who I believe was the ship's captain. He looked smart in his crisp white uniform, which had lots of different medals, badges, gold buttons and a buckle belt and looked very ornate. The sailors, too, wore white uniforms, with slightly less of what the captain had on his clothing, but equally smart. As they stood regimented in line, they held their heads up high on guard.

Standing on the ship, it felt scary and unstable, and I wondered how it remained on water. I kept wanting to look down, but the height was frightening. We were led into chambers, which seemed cramped and really small. I thought, *how can they live and work in this space?* It felt claustrophobic and I wasn't sure I liked it! I couldn't imagine Mum and Dad being on a ship.

However, it was an experience that I'll never forget. As we left the ship, we were each given foreign chocolates by some of the sailors: yum yum!

# Chapter 4
# A Turning Point

We had been at the convent for eighteen months when two of Mum's sisters came to visit. They were my godmother Collette and Auntie Liseby, from England. Liseby didn't look familiar and nor did she look typically Mauritian, with her fair skin and jet-black hair. Her cheeky smile made her even more attractive, and she wore fashionable clothes. I couldn't stop staring at her, studying every detail, from her earrings to the shoes she wore. She told us all about where they lived in London, making it sound as though it was a country, because it sounded big and inviting. She explained the difficulties Mum and Dad faced from the time they arrived in Europe, and how they were separated for some time, but things were improving, and we would soon be able to reunite. Surprise, surprise, we had two more additions to the family: brother Peter and sister Jaqueline. It made me smile and I couldn't wait to meet them both. How they managed that during their separation, I'll never know.

As we listened, none of us understood the legalities surrounding Dad's actions. I was simply listening to a daring story that made him appear brave, of how he entered the UK illegally, acting on the advice given to him by a work colleague, who suggested that he dressed to blend in, and appear as a travelling businessman. He had the works: top hat, striped suit, umbrella in one hand and a briefcase in the other. Travelling via Marseilles to Ireland, from there he made his way to London Victoria. The plan worked. He wasn't asked to produce a passport at any of the borders he crossed, which I guess was pure luck. I could imagine Dad pulling this off, as he always appeared confident and his sharp dress sense would have certainly helped with this plan.

That, then, is how he was able to gain entry and finally be reunited with Mum. However, it later became clear had this plan not worked, the consequence would have been terrible for him and his family.

Auntie Liseby also gave us the good news that Gert would soon be leaving to join them in London. Although I was happy for her, I can't lie; I felt disappointed that it wasn't me and questioned why this was the case. They explained that it was to do with the airfare, which was cheaper for a child under the age of twelve. One month before Gert's twelfth birthday, she left the convent and travelled alone to England.

We experienced many changes that year. Soon after Gert left, Marie went to stay at Aunt Denise's place to help with the daily chores and look after our cousins. That same year, Cecile and I moved up to the elders' dormitory, then Mireille was transferred from the crèche into the main building. Her dormitory was where we slept on the first floor. It was nice, because we got to know her a little more, and she in turn felt safer knowing we were there to help her adjust.

At times, the odd family member would visit us for an hour or so, mainly on Sunday afternoons, which we looked forward to. We'd always be told who was coming to visit, and would sit and wait patiently on the long concrete bench in front of the chapel. It faced the entrance, so we could see those coming through. I loved Sundays, purely because it meant treats and seeing the family, but as the months passed, we saw less and less of them.

I was sad for some of the girls who never had any visitors, especially girls like Ursulle. I'd always make sure they shared my treats, because it simply gave me joy to see the happiness on their faces, as it was a rare thing in the convent. Growing up, I remember having a sense of pleasure whenever I had something to give, to see the reaction and appreciation, which made me feel I was doing some good.

There were the odd couples and visitors who simply came along to donate toys and give treats to the underprivileged orphans. One Sunday afternoon, I was expecting a visit from Collette, but she was late. Time was running out before visiting hours were over. However, a young couple noticed me sitting all alone. They came over and asked for my name, and introduced themselves as Michelle and Robert. They seemed kind and handed me a bag of boiled sweets. I told them my godmother hadn't arrived, and seeing the sadness on my face they gave me some reassuring words, telling me they would come and visit me, too.

This couple didn't have children of their own. They were just kind and wanted to spread love and joy. I was comforted to know that I'd always have visitors, and sure enough, they came near enough every Sunday, with more treats. On a number of occasions they'd ask permission to take me out to the park, and you can imagine my excitement when this happened. I truly grew close to them both, for they showed me care and affection I hadn't experienced before.

A few months later, on a Sunday after mass, Mère Supérieure Seraphine asked me to wait in the chapel, as she needed to speak with me. I thought I was in trouble, but she sat me down and gave me a reassuring smile, which I thought was odd, as she rarely did that. She explained that a couple had made a request to adopt me, which meant I'd have to go and live with them.

Without hesitation, I replied, 'Yes. Will it be Michelle's place?'

She replied, 'Of course! Who else?'

The idea of leaving the convent was all I could think of, plus they were nice to me. However, she explained there might be some difficulties, because Mum and Dad were still alive. The convent had a duty to inform them and ask for permission. I remember shrugging my shoulders to suggest I didn't mind. I was just so happy that someone wanted me to be part of their family.

As the months passed, I prayed religiously that I could go and live with Michelle, but heard nothing. Then one day Collette came to visit, and told me that Mum and Dad did not agree to the adoption, and plans were in place for some of us to be reunited with them. I felt better, because there was some hope that I'd soon leave this place, no matter what. Of course, Michelle and Robert were disappointed, but happy for me to soon be with my proper family.

Back in the UK, after years of appeal, both Mum and Dad finally managed to get their papers in order to legalise their immigration status, which enabled them to start the job of reuniting the family. He had made contact with an individual in the Mauritian community who offered help and advice to those struggling to settle in the UK. The community would organise regular fund-raising events, at social gatherings in Leicester Square. After hearing Dad's story and of how he was potentially losing his children to adoption, they agreed to ease the burden by offering him an interest-free loan to fund our passage.

It was a weekday when we received an unexpected visit from two aunties, together with Marie and my younger brother Jean Marc. I hadn't seen him since we were separated at Maraine's place. He was all grown up, and seemed quiet and withdrawn, as though he didn't know us. They told us that we would soon be joining Mum and Dad in England.

Before travelling in October, we needed to be vaccinated. The five of us – Marie, Cecile, Liseby, Jean Marc and me – accompanied by Aunt Collette and Denise made the twenty-minute walk into the capital. I must have skipped all the way to the clinic and back; even the dreaded needle didn't faze me. We were each given two injections, but would have to come back for another in a week, which in my mind couldn't come quick enough.

October came, with the good news that we were finally leaving, I jumped for joy, and rushed to tell my friends. Somehow Ursulle didn't seem happy, but I told her that I'd see her again one day. I asked her to let me take one of her dolls, convincing her that it would go somewhere better than the convent, but it wasn't going to be that easy. I tried to snatch it from her, and ended up fighting on the landing, at the top of the stairs that led into the courtyard. With one shove, I managed to grab the doll, but it caused her to trip and she fell down several steps, still panting heavily. I gasped in horror!

Her screams still haunt me. I didn't realise at the time she'd broken her arm, but was more worried that she had ripped her tights, which instantly meant facing punishment. As she lay on the ground, crying in agony, I repeatedly shouted across: 'I didn't mean it! I'm sorry!'

I even promised to buy her new tights (although realistically, at the time, I didn't know how that was going to pan out!). Growing up, I learnt the importance of a promise and how bad it can leave you feeling if it's not kept. Not honouring this would not sit well with me.

Her continuing cries scared me even more, so I ran down the steps to hand the doll back. Mère Supérieure Seraphine and a few girls hurried over to see the commotion, and seeing this I ran off in hiding, thinking that my punishment would mean that I couldn't leave the convent. I hid in the toilet and cried and cried. In the distance I could hear Sister Du Calvert calling out my name in search. I had never been so frightened or worried about the circumstances.

When they eventually caught up with me, the punishment was a caning never to be forgotten. I was sent to the chapel to pray for forgiveness and given no food that evening. The next day, I saw Ursulle's arm in plaster. She wouldn't look at me, let alone speak to me. I gave her a bar of chocolate, and told her how sorry I was and that I would keep my promise to come back to see her one day. She shrugged a shoulder, still with no words, and I believe she secretly hoped it could happen. Although that's what I wanted to happen, I didn't know what I was really promising, and in reality I was totally unaware of how difficult it would be.

You can imagine my excitement over the next few days. Sunday arrived, and as promised, Michelle and Robert came to visit, this time to say farewell. I wasn't looking forward to that part. They gave me their address, asking me to write. I couldn't give them mine, as I didn't know myself where I was going. I promised to tell them all about my new life in England. Michelle gave me a package containing a pretty yellow polka-dot dress made from sheer organza. She told me to wear it to travel, as it was special. As we said our goodbyes, they held me so tight. Deep down I felt their sadness, as I waved them goodbye. I tried hard not to cry. I had mixed emotions, knowing I'd never forget them.

I counted the days to us leaving. The path ahead wasn't clear, but I felt it couldn't be worse than where we were at. I tried to picture England, but found it difficult. The English books I read in class were all Greek to me. I never understood a word of what was written. You could say I was, well, uneducated. It was impossible to imagine the English way of life from simply watching *Top of the Pops* and seeing the fashion magazines that Monique had lying around.

My last night in the convent was the most exciting. Ursulle and I sat up giggling and talking about where I was going. She told me she'd never forget me, because of the experience of a broken arm. I had hoped that it would be because she valued me as a friend, but who could blame her; after all, I was trying to tear her family away. I felt bad for her and gave her all my personal belongings, which I couldn't take, as we were to travel light.

Although I didn't get much sleep that night, I woke up for the first time without hesitation. We were being picked up straight after mass. Marie and Auntie Collette arrived, and we all went to the crèche to say goodbye to Shirley. She didn't really understand what was happening, it was horrible leaving her behind.

As we were leaving, some children and nuns were lined up outside the chapel to wave us goodbye, Ursulle stayed at the back, and I'm certain she was crying. Inside I felt I had let her down somehow. Mireille had made friends with Matunga. A nun was trying to console her, as she couldn't stop crying. Apart from the waving, I can't remember actually speaking to any of the nuns or priests about leaving, and nor do I remember looking back at any of them in case they stopped us from going; but I clearly remember that seeing the back of that awful place was the best feeling ever.

We went back to Maraine's place where Jean Marc was waiting. We had a quick lunch with the family, then everything happened really quickly: more goodbyes, before leaving for the hour journey to Plaisance airport. I remember feeling very nervous about getting on the aeroplane. We quickly had to say our final goodbyes to those who accompanied us, who wished us luck (maybe they knew we might need it). We were left in the capable hands of a pretty air hostess, who chaperoned us throughout the terminal and across into customs. Then we walked across the tarmac, seeing the big aeroplane. The loud whirring sound scared me even more. I remember walking up the steps to enter this enormous machine – not to mention that the thought of it taking us up into the sky was even more daunting. I felt vulnerable and unsafe.

We were taken to our seats, where I was glad I was by the window. The air hostess buckled us all in, then I listened carefully to the continuous announcement and the chimes that alerted and advised passengers of what was happening. Luckily these were in both French and English.

When it was time, the plane taxied across the tarmac. I remember thinking it was too slow, but then it stopped for a while, before picking up speed again in preparation for lift off.

None of us spoke, and nor did we know what to expect. I could feel the rattling and bumps as the plane picked up speed then lifted into the air at an angle, pushing us back in our seats. I grabbed hold of Marie's hands, who was just as nervous as the rest of us.

Once in the air, I tried to get a glimpse of the clouds that I so admired as a child. I was amazed that the plane was just cutting through them, which puzzled me. Looking down below, I could see the outline of our small island, surrounded by the vast ocean, which caused me to feel a certain sadness. Could it be I'd never see the vision I had as a child that day in the water?

It wasn't long after take-off that the pressure caused our ears to hurt. We were given sweets and a drink. The noise was deafening, making it difficult to hear anything. The food came in a foil tray that smelt unfamiliar and tasted horrible. For a brief moment, I missed the food back at the convent. I was feeling cold and uncomfortable, wearing only a thin dress, which didn't help.

The journey was taking too long. I kept asking the others whether we'd arrived yet. Marie got fed up.

After a dozen or so times, she said, 'We'll be there tomorrow,' just to shut me up.

I don't think she knew herself how long the journey was going to take. As it turned out, it was a fifteen-hour flight.

I slept through the tiring journey, but quickly woke up at the sound of the pilot's voice over the Tannoy, announcing we were soon to land. The sensation and mechanical noise associated with the descent was just as bad as the take-off. However, when the tyres bounced off the tarmac it felt as though we had crashed. I'm sure I heard some screams. My heart was beating fast from nerves and the uncertainty of what lay before us.

We landed at Stansted airport. The oval window was misty, but I tried to get a glimpse of the outside. It was dark and raining. We were the last to leave the plane, accompanied by the same friendly air hostess. As we left the plane, we shivered as we walked down the steps. We were all wearing light clothing and the cold pierced us like a knife.

From the moment I arrived at the terminal, everything seemed foreign, from a language that I couldn't understand, to the smell. The rain was miserable, not as welcoming as back home, where it cooled us down from the heat. The contrast in climate was something I was not prepared for. In my mind I imagined Mum and Dad meeting us on the tarmac, but it didn't happen like that. We didn't have any luggage with us, save for Marie, who'd carried a large statue of the Virgin Mary on her lap throughout the flight.

We then arrived in the airport lounge, where there were many people waiting, some carrying names on large placards. A tall gentleman was holding one of these with our surname written on it. As we approached him, he spoke to us in French and introduced himself as Monsieur Marcel. He explained that Dad had gone to the wrong airport, which was miles from where we were, and because it was late, we were to go with him to his place and would see them the next day. Naturally, we were all disappointed, but we were too tired to care. We just wanted to be somewhere warm.

I didn't understand English and even the French language seemed difficult, because I'd got so used to speaking Creole. I felt like a fish out of water. Tired from the long journey, I just wanted to close my eyes, but as I looked out of the car window, I was amazed by all the bright sparkling lights inside the tall buildings, which lit up like a magical world. Stupidly, I thought we might see a beach or the sea on the horizon, just like you would if you were travelling on the coast back home.

My tummy was rumbling with hunger pains and I looked across at the others to see if they felt the same. No one was speaking, but it was obvious that we all felt cold, anxious and nervous. When we arrived at his house, I thought it would be lovely inside, but the rooms were small and cramped. We were

41

introduced to his wife, a sweet lady who offered us tea and toast with butter and jam. I had never tasted anything like it before; it was yummy! We all enjoyed it very much.

Before going to bed, we shared a few stories about our experience in the convent. It was sad to hear about my brother's life at the boys' convent. I thought we had it bad, but their experience was no better.

The next morning, we got ready. Our breakfast was the same toasted bread and jam. Madame Marcel spoke to us in French:

*'Je sais que vous ne pouvez pas encore parlais anglais, mais il y a deux mots bien importants que vous devez apprendre rapidement: c'est s'il vous plaît et merci! Quand même, ses mots sont très polis, méfié les Anglais ne sont pas si gentile.'*

('I know you can't speak English yet, but there are two important words that you need to learn fast, and that's please, and thank you. Although these are very polite words, beware English people are not that friendly.')

I was a little taken aback by this and did not yet understand what was meant by it.

Realising we had no other clothing, she gave us cardigans and jumpers to wear that were way too big, but we were all thankful. Excited and nervous to see Mum and Dad, we walked for about fifteen minutes until in the distance we could see them both. I didn't know how to react. Part of me wanted to run and give them a hug and maybe a kiss, but it didn't come naturally. I wanted Dad to see that I was brave and did not show any emotions of pain – or at least that's what I thought I should do. If I'm not mistaken, I believe Marie and the others greeted them, but I stayed still. They were speaking to us in a mixture of French and Creole, but I only replied in Creole. Although they would have been surprised by this, no remark was made.

We walked a further twenty minutes to Grandmother's place. Although, a short distance, the cold made it almost impossible. On arrival, we stood in front of this tall building, a skyscraper called Durrington Tower in Wandsworth Road. It had a lift, which none of us had ever seen or used before. Some of us hesitated and were reluctant to use it, and once inside it felt claustrophobic. It made a terrible noise and had a strong stench of urine.

The flat was on the fifteenth floor. As the heavy metal door opened, we could see Gert waiting for us on the doorstep. She was trying to manage a toddler who was running around, the brother we heard about back home, Peter.

Gert welcomed us with a big smile, and spoke really fast in English, basically showing off. I didn't understand a word of what she said. Inside we met the rest of the family, Eric looked the same, but taller. He was all grown up and looked smart. It was nice to see the beautiful Aunt Liseby who came to visit us in Mauritius. I was too young to remember my grandmother Anita when she left Mauritius. She was a little lady, with a sweet smile. She didn't speak much, but appeared kind. She was busying herself in the kitchen. Her other sons, Corneille and Henri, were there, too.

It was a big family reunion with lots of food and drinks. Everyone was sharing jokes, laughing and speaking over one another, as Mauritians do, with no filter. I remember feeling very tired and in need of sleep. We all stayed at the flat that night, sleeping on various mattresses laid out on the floor, sharing beds with my other sisters. It was utter chaos, but we were happy.

The next day, we took a bus and travelled to where Mum and Dad were renting a place in Stoke Newington. On the way they stopped to buy us some warmer clothes. The place was far from nice, but we didn't complain; it was simply lovely to be reunited with the family again, not to mention leaving that horrible place behind. I felt free from danger, and nothing else could ever hurt me, or so I thought.

# Chapter 5
# Culture Shock

Mum would speak about Shirley. She expressed her sorrow for leaving us behind, and from the low tone in her voice you could feel the guilt eating away at her. I told as much as I could, about how she'd grown and the time spent with her in the crèche.

There were still four children left behind. She explained why they couldn't afford to send for us all, mentioning their concern of adoption led them to borrow money to pay for five of us to come. Mum felt it was important to explain their plans to send for the others, once they found a suitable place, with enough money saved.

She asked about the family who wanted to adopt me. I told her I had their address and would write to them, but as soon as I mentioned this I realised I didn't know where I'd left it. I must have mislaid it in the commotion of travelling. I felt bad. The idea of breaking a promise exposed me as a person not to be trusted and, worse, I had failed. I couldn't bear to ask Mum to help me find it, as she was already feeling bad herself.

Mum continued working at the bakery. Initially Dad found it hard to find work, but after making friends within the Mauritian community, one person in particular (who worked at Whipps Cross Hospital in Walthamstow) helped find him a job as a porter, where he worked for several years.

We lived in Stoke Newington for about a year. I can't say I remember much about the place, but I will always hold dear the memory of Mum taking us to the cinema for the first time. The film was *The Sound of Music*, with Julie Andrews. Even though it was hard to understand the language, the storyline was clear.

Like us, the family simply loved music. I felt the film was based on us, and from then on we considered ourselves the Von Trapp family; there were far too many similarities.

Our first school in England was St Thomas More in Wood Green. This is where it would become clear what Madame Marcel had meant when she told us how unkind British people can be. I'd already turned twelve on my first day at school, and I looked smart in my navy-blue uniform as I stood at the school gates with Gert, who was already attending there. The school playground was huge with lots of children playing. Gert explained a few things about what I should do, and as the bell rang everybody started scattering around, Gert included, and headed for the main building. I followed and entered a large assembly hall. Everybody was sitting close together on the floor, with crossed legs.

I found myself next to a boy, who frowned at me, as if to say, 'What are you looking at? Or 'Who are you?' I smiled, but he made me feel like a weirdo, pulling himself away as though I was contagious. He was whispering to another lad sat next to him, but kept looking over at me, I got the impression that he wanted me to say something, but I stayed quiet. He was goading me to speak.

Then one lad asked, 'Are you a Paki?'

I didn't understand what he said, so I simply grinned. He obviously didn't like my reaction, and smacked me hard on the arm. Shocked at what had just happened, I put my head down and wanted to cry, although I was angry inside. Some of the children sitting nearby giggled at what they'd just seen, I felt vulnerable and became a target that day. In the corridors, other children stared at me in the same way, making me feel unwelcome.

I found my class and sat in silence throughout. The teacher spoke to me at the end of class, only to realise my lack of English.

He took me to the headmaster's office, where words were exchanged, but I didn't know what was being said.

As I walked into class the next day, the teacher called me outside, and took me to another class with much younger children in. There I was at the age of twelve, sitting with Year 2 children, aged between six and seven. It didn't help that I struggled with the language.

I remember having to select a book, and for homework I needed to write an essay about my understanding of the story. It was to be the first English book I ever read, called *The Pearl*. I chose it for two reasons: the cover reminded me of back home, and it was small. Being put into a lower class gave reason for the bullying to continue. I felt isolated and left out by other pupils. I couldn't make any friends, and my confidence and self-esteem were worn down by the bullies.

It was mainly the boys who did the name-calling and bullying. I kept to myself as much as I could, but they'd always find me in a corner somewhere. I didn't want to learn or go to school, which impeded me academically, and as a result suffered a lack of communication. I lived like this for a year, and there were times I wished I was back with my friends in the convent.

Our landlord wanted to increase the rent, which made it financially difficult, so Mum and Dad looked for a cheaper place to rent. Not long afterwards, we moved to a privately rented one-bedroom furnished flat in Stamford Hill, North London. It was a large house converted into flats. We all had to share one large bedroom, with a small kitchen and separate toilet. The set-up was weird. There were mattresses laid out on the floor, a double bed, a pram, where baby Jacqueline spent most of her time, and a small cot in the corner for Peter. It was so cramped I couldn't see how it was going to work, but it did. I'm sure the people living upstairs would have found us annoying, as we were a noisy lot, and used to sing for entertainment. We rarely went out to play. We did, however, have a colour TV, which to us was pure luxury.

Marie's love for cleaning was obsessive. One day, when cleaning a large window, she awkwardly knocked her knees and cut herself badly. I'd never seen so much blood. It was like a crime scene! She had to have a number of stitches in hospital.

There was a lot of activity outside the place we lived in. The main road was a busy one lined with many shops, and it was noisy, to say the least. I couldn't help noticing that many men were wearing black suits, with a fringed garment, black hats and long coats. They had the strangest long, curly locks that fell at the side of their faces, and although the colour of their skin was white they somehow behaved and looked different from other English people. I later learned that they were Jewish and we lived in a large Jewish community. I was beginning to understand the existence of various nationalities and cultures, and it helped to know that we weren't the only foreigners living in this foreign land.

The overcrowding meant the family could now apply for a council property. Given our ages, some of us needed our own rooms. News came in that we were soon moving into a three-bedroom house on Amhurst Road in Hackney Downs. The large corner house was divided into two separate apartments. Our friendly neighbours upstairs were the Andersons, a Jamaican couple with a disabled daughter. The apartment was much bigger. It had two floors, with a large kitchen, a dining area, and a downstairs lounge; upstairs were two large bedrooms, and a box room, which Eric occupied. The babies Jacqueline and Peter shared Mum and Dad's room. The other large room had bunk beds, which six of us had to share. It was laid out like a dormitory. As usual, Marie kept it clean, and would encourage us to do the same. We made our own beds in the morning, and took it in turns to do different chores around the house. Our time in the convent certainly helped with this.

We quickly settled in our new place. Although I was happy to leave the last school, you could say I wasn't looking forward to going to the new one, Edith Cavell School on Kingsland Road, Dalston. Coincidently, the girls' convent was on a road with the same name. Our school uniform wasn't as nice as the last one. It was maroon in colour, but I didn't mind. I hoped it was going to be a better place to study.

I had been at the school a few days when I made my first friend in England. Her name was Alma and she was in the same year. Originally from Jamaica, she spoke English with a heavy Jamaican accent that at first was difficult for me to understand, given my lack of English. However, we managed to communicate somehow. Alma was tall and shy. She didn't have many friends. You could say she wasn't very popular, but she was intelligent and good at sports. On the other hand, I hated sports, especially hockey. I always made some excuse not to take part.

Alma would often help me with my homework, and having her as a friend eased the settling in. I started to enjoy going to school and was feeling good about it, until something happened.

We were given free school meals in the canteen. While I was sitting on my own in the dining hall, a group of girls approached me and asked for money. Being poor, pocket money was a rare thing. I told them I didn't have any, and one of the girls decided to scoop some food from my tray and rub it in my hair.

At the same time, another threatened me, saying, 'We're gonna rough you up after school.'

Confused, I wasn't sure exactly what they meant, but it didn't sound friendly. I told Alma what took place and she explained how nasty some of the girls at this school could be, and said I should keep to myself and just ignore it, hoping it wouldn't happen. Still wary, I became anxious about the possibility and didn't know what to do.

That very afternoon on my way home, walking out of the gates I noticed the same group of girls outside. I tried to avoid them by

48

walking away, but they followed me out of the gates. Once outside, without warning they grabbed my bag and pulled at my hair, taking it in turns to hit, punch and kick me. The biggest girl got hold of my ponytail and started swinging me around like a rag doll. I felt my hair being pulled from the roots. It was painful.

This public assault was happening on a busy main road, and no one stopped to help. After a while I thought, *just let them finish doing what they want to do*. I was outnumbered, not that I knew how to fight back. I knew they'd have to stop at some stage, so I bravely took the knocks, thinking all the time, *I am not going to cry*. I was not going to give them the satisfaction of seeing me in pain.

The trauma seemed never-ending, then I heard one of them say, 'I think she's had enough for now – but you'd better have some bread next time we see you, you Paki!'

Then they giggled and walked away, leaving me kneeling on the pavement near the school entrance, with a bleeding lip. My face and head hurt badly. My hair had been ruffled up and my uniform was torn. I looked a total mess. Out of sight of the girls, I started to cry, thinking, *how am I going to explain this to Mum? And steal bread at breakfast to take to school the next day!* Or so I thought that was what the bullies meant, I later found out the term bread meant money...

I slowly limped back home. Once indoors, I don't know why, but I didn't tell anyone about it. Part of me felt embarrassed for having been beaten up, not to mention these girls managed to destroy any self-esteem I had. I was in shock. The assault was so public, which was even more traumatic for me.

I didn't want to go back to school but I knew I had to. Still in pain, I skipped school the next day. No one at home questioned the way I looked, even though my face was all puffed up and my lip was cut in two places. Mum simply thought I wasn't well. They were always busy working and parenting the other children that I don't think they even noticed my pain.

I was starting to realise how cruel people can be in this world. You didn't just get punished in a convent; people in general can also become an enemy. I built up a certain anger after this event, but at the same time it opened my eyes to the dangers around me. I needed to control my fears and hide my vulnerability in order to survive. Ironically, back home, being fair made me a target at school, but in England to some I was seen as a Paki, which I later learnt was a racist term used towards Indian people. Certain individuals didn't always like dark-skinned foreigners, which obviously I was in their eyes; this confused me even more. I quickly learned more and more about the shocking contrast between cultures.

The experience caused me to hate school. I couldn't concentrate on my studies; I became an introvert and isolated myself. My worst subjects were Maths and English. I did, however, enjoy French, which was second nature, Religious Studies, and Drama, because it involved music. By the time I reached Fifth Form, kids in French lessons seemed friendlier. I think they saw me as someone who could help them with their homework. At times, I let my barrier down, which allowed me to make new friends. The boys in class would flirt with me; they thought I was French because of my name and heavy accent. One in particular was a lad named Paul. He was Jewish and good looking. I'd say he was shy, but girls adored him. I, too, had a secret crush on him. He always sat next to me in class. I helped him with French, he seemed comfortable around me, but we never became anything other than friends. Flirting at school was interesting. Girls would become my friends simply because they wanted to be noticed by the boys who were giving me attention.

There were some funny moments, like the time the school asked families to contribute towards food hampers for harvest. A few of us would deliver these to deserving pensioners struggling to make ends meet. I convinced my group that I knew a family who would benefit from it, so they delivered a hamper straight to my home, as I hid, watching from a distance.

During summer breaks, we'd be palmed off for a week or so to extended relatives, either singularly or in twos, just to give Mum and Dad a break, and of course it was nice for us, too. Realistically, the family couldn't afford to take us on holiday, so we'd make the most of our short trips away. I especially enjoyed staying with an aunt and her husband who lived in Aberystwyth, Wales. They didn't have children of her own, so I was spoilt rotten, with new clothes and sweet treats, and visits to some amazing places. In fact, I was treated like a princess. I particularly loved Tenby beach, which took me back to my homeland.

In the 70s, Hackney and various parts of East London became a centre where many West Indians lived. Walking out in the street, you'd often hear reggae music blaring from people's homes. I loved the rhythm and beat of reggae music. At times, our neighbour upstairs would invite us older girls to various house parties. They were decent people, and Mum and Dad trusted them to look out for us. We'd walk into a dimly lit room down in a crowded basement, where the heat was unbearable, with music blaring from large speakers in every corner of the room. Watching people smooching in corners, Marie and I stood around, trying to understand the set-up.

It was to be the first time I'd be asked to dance. A tall man in his thirties and wearing a colourful Hawaiian shirt, which was undone to reveal his gleaming bare chest, approached me with open arms, inviting me to dance by grabbing my hands, before thrusting me against his sweaty torso. The dance moves were awkward and uncomfortable. It was nothing like I'd seen before. It felt as though both his feet were stuck on chewing gum, whilst trying to grind up against me. The excessive sweating mixed with Old Spice aftershave and a strong smell of alcohol was not appealing.

Pulling myself away from him, I said, 'I want to dance this way,' jiggling my body see-saw style, trying to stick to the beat.

Looking around, I realised I was the odd one out. He walked off in a huff, whilst I kept jiggling side to side, faster than the beat of the music.

Mum was working two jobs, as well as juggling a household of nine children. By December 1972, they managed to save enough money to bring over two of our brothers from back home. By then, Bernard was seven and Popol was eight. Had it not been for Eric, who helped finance their fares, their reunion would have been further delayed. At the age of fifteen, as well as studying, Eric worked in a hotel kitchen in the evenings to help the household financially. He'd ride his bike at night and sometimes bring back leftovers for us to eat. One night on his way home, he was stopped by the police, who found a large amount of food in his bag. After questioning him, the officer took him home. He knocked on our door in the early hours, and gave Dad a talking to for letting his young son out at night this way! It shouldn't have happened and we knew it wasn't ideal, but we had to muck in and help bring extra money in to help where we could.

In our mid-teens, myself and Gert also took on part-time jobs at weekends and at times after school. On Saturdays, I worked at the local Wimpy bar to help with food shopping. After school, we'd be left caring for the younger ones, when Mum went to work in the Matchbox toy factory. She often brought back small toy cars for us to play with. At night, she worked as a cleaner at a Barclays bank in the city. This went on for a number of years.

On our way to school, we would take the babies Peter and Jacqueline to a babysitter. I always remember the day it snowed heavily overnight, leaving twelve inches of snow on the ground. Pushing Jacqueline in the pram was hard work and we struggled. None of us could see the road surface for the snow, and we hit the mount of pavement with force, resulting in the pram catapulting Jacqueline, who was all wrapped up in a white blanket, straight out of her pram. She landed buried into the white snow. Shocked at the sight, we thought we had killed her; but with delayed laughter we all found it hilarious and laughed all the way to the babysitter.

There were many mishaps like these when we cared for the toddlers. Once we had taken Peter to the park in his pushchair. Being kids ourselves, we were keen to go on the swings and left the pram in front where we could see him, but he decided to come out and run towards us. Obviously, he too wanted to have fun. With the swing moving at speed, it was too late to stop. It smashed him straight in the face, causing him to fall and cut his lip badly. A witness quickly called an ambulance, which took him to the hospital for treatment. Mum did not hear the last of it from the authorities, and I am sure it made the local news, too! These events proved dangerous, forcing Mum to stop working during the day.

**Mum and Dad's wedding picture**

**Dad and his family**

**Grandad
on Dad's side**

**Our home on the Establishment**

**The Chateaux**

The local Tabaje

The last picture taken as children before being separated to go into boys' and girls' convents. Starting from the back, left to right: Cecile, Danielle, Marie, Gertrude, Francois, Bernard, Popol, Mireille and Jean Marc.

**Uncles and sugar cane workers enjoying a drink to
celebrate the harvest**

**The girls' convent**

**Myself, Gertrude, Mireille and our cousin Helen as bridesmaids for Stella and Fanfan's wedding**

**Myself, Cecile and Mireille with others in the convent**

**Dad in his favourite suit**

**Our house in Hackney**

**My early days at Edith Cavell School in London**

# Chapter 6
# Beautiful Chaos

François was reunited with us. Our household was growing in numbers, which meant one thing: chaos! However, Shirley had left the convent to stay at Maraine's place. In 1972, the family was complete when she joined us, by which time she was six years old. Understandably, she found it difficult to settle. We were total strangers to her, so she didn't know or recognise anyone. Shy and quiet, we heard she didn't want to leave Monique, as she had grown close to her. On a number of occasions, she insisted Mum and Dad weren't her real parents. Still in the habit of sucking her thumb, you'd see her rocking herself back and forth in comfort whilst asleep or sitting in a corner somewhere.

Mum and Dad had to live with the guilt of leaving us behind. In their minds, it was a small sacrifice to pay for what should have been temporary, rightly or wrongly. A lot of their plans were out of their control, from Mum being ill to their immigration status, all of which made it difficult for us to be reunited. Nevertheless, their hard work was starting to pay off, even given that Mum had never worked back home. Between them, they survived by focusing on being a family again. Despite working two or three jobs at a time, living in a foreign land, dealing with the language barrier, difference in culture, and living in squalid conditions, neither of them moaned. They just got on with the job of reuniting us, to continue where they left off, doing their best as parents.

We were to face many more challenges before we could individually achieve a better quality of life. Being detached from our parents affected us all in one way or another. For some, like Shirley, the effect was immediate. She distanced herself from all of us and it was obvious she was homesick. She often cried, asking to return back home.

Our house was always hectic. Although poor, we were rich in fun and laughter. Mum and Dad hosted many family gatherings at home. With thirteen children, this was no surprise; come to think of it, there was a birthday to celebrate every month. Mum was pregnant for almost fifteen years of her life and had a child nearly every year from 1954 to 1969, with a break here and there. Being part of a large extended family meant there'd be many other parties going on every month, and these gatherings kept us closely knit as a family.

It was natural for Mum to nurture. Dad, too, had a heart of gold. He'd give you his last penny and the shirt off his back if he could. If you came to visit, he wasn't happy unless you had a drink and a plate of food in front of you. That's how he expressed his appreciation and love for people. Even though they didn't use loving words to express themselves, they both genuinely loved and cared for us all.

The family was poor and living on the breadline, but they didn't steal or beg. They relied on doorstep loans to cope with birthdays and Christmas, from organisations that were initially very happy to loan you money and were friendly at first. When things got tight it showed in Mum's demeanour, as though she carried the world on her shoulders, but she never made us feel guilty for borrowing money from the likes of The Provident and Shopacheck. Mr Barrie would often appear on our doorstep and I'd say he was one of the nice ones. He took pity on Mum and would allow her more time to pay up. No doubt he could see the worry on her face when she'd stand at the door in her light blue quilted dressing gown.

Most of our clothes were hand-me-downs from extended family. I got given a pair of shoes that caused my toes to press through the leather, and I'm sure I wasn't the only one who suffered a wardrobe malfunction. More important items, like school uniforms, would come from the Littlewoods catalogue. After being worn for a while, they would be passed down before Mum could even finish paying for them.

Mum controlled the purse strings. Dad would hand over 90% of his weekly earnings for housekeeping, and Mum would carefully put some aside to prioritise house bills and make sure we were fed. She never went out socially with friends. In fact, back then Mum would never be seen in a pub. However, Dad would enjoy the odd lunchtime tipple at the local pub, which was literally opposite our house. Several days a week he'd have a flutter on the dogs and horse racing at the local bookmakers. He did so for many years, but always set himself a limit, wagering small amounts at a time. He was totally faithful to Mum, and betting was the only love affair he ever had. It was more of a social thing for him, as he enjoyed the male interaction and it took him away from the chaos at home.

None of us had friends that came home; a sleepover was unheard of in our culture. We had to entertain ourselves, often putting on a cabaret show at home, giving us an excuse to sing and dance. Like us, Monique influenced Shirley's singing talent. Our family cabaret was the only time she ever involved herself. Eric was too busy with work and studies, and Popol thought he was too cool, and truly believed he'd be the next James Bond. Potentially, he had the looks, but remained in the background. You could say he took himself seriously. I guess he didn't want to be ridiculed.

Mauritians never need an excuse to party and weekly family gatherings are part of the culture. Mum would make a large dish of biryani or a curry for all to share, and the guests would contribute with drinks and snacks. You'd always see a bottle of whisky and rum on the table. It was exciting, as we enjoyed rearranging the dining area, positioning chairs set out in one big circle.

Without a doubt, it meant providing the evening entertainment, with songs, and sketches we'd rehearse to perfection. Marie and I would sing a harmonious duet to our favourite songs. One in particular was 'To Know, Know, Know Him'. Jean Marc was a natural comedian. He was always spot on when imitating others in the family. We'd spend hours laughing at his antics.

We challenged ourselves in talent competitions. Jean Marc would use any household objects he could find to play the drums. Serving spoon in hands, we'd sing alone or pretend we were a band. Some of us took it seriously and others did it for a laugh, especially when out of tune. The younger ones like Jacqueline would sit back and watch. Little did she know this would be her career one day.

Mum had a beautiful soft-toned voice. At times, she'd sing French songs, hitting the high notes as a soprano and surprising everybody with her hidden talents. After a few bevvies, Dad would find the confidence to blurt out his favourite song: 'Please Release Me' by Engelbert Humperdinck. We didn't understand the meaning of these words until much later in life. Was he trying to tell Mum something? Makes you wonder! He'd also spend ages sharing bad jokes from his time in Mauritius. They weren't always funny, but we laughed to humour him.

My sisters and I were often bridesmaids, which we didn't mind as it meant a party, with new clothes and decent food to eat. Mealtimes when you're poor are not the best. At breakfast, Mum would toast a whole loaf of bread and spread the slices with lashings of Stork margarine, as we couldn't afford the real thing. We'd dip the bread in the tea, leaving melted butter floating in the mugs, yuck! Our hungry tummies didn't prevent us from tucking in! Mum would also reheat leftover food that Eric bought back from the hotel and serve it for dinner.

Dad took care of the shopping, and we'd often hear him say, 'Nou al débrouiller' ('Let's go and scramble'). He'd take a couple of us along to Ridley Road Market in Dalston in time for when the stalls were packing up, as many old fruits would be discarded as rubbish. Sometimes we'd buy bags of bruised ones on the cheap, which the sellers just wanted to get rid of.

Back in the 70s, it was common to see children playing on the streets. The lack of traffic and very different attitudes gave kids a sense of freedom, which is quite remote now. My younger siblings were no different. They'd be out playing handstands against the side wall or joyriding the neighbour's bike (but would always put it back). Although we appeared a dysfunctional family, we were generally well behaved. Even though we argued at times, swearing and physical fighting was never encouraged – apart from an incident involving Cecile. She was generally reserved, but if rubbed up the wrong way, she'd demonstrate her hidden temper. Whilst playing out, she was being picked on and bullied by a local girl, and François came running in to tell Mum what was happening. I'll never forget the speed Mum ran out of the house, her apron still tied to her. She was a little on the heavy side, and without questioning, with all her might she pulled this girl away from Cecile. Grabbing hold of her hair, she spun her around and threw her to the ground. The girl quickly got up and ran off, never to be seen again! We watched in stunned amazement at the way Mum had reacted. I guess it was a mother's instinct to protecting her child.

I spent most of my time watching TV after school, apart from listening to music, my favourite programmes were, *Crossroads* as it helped me learn how to pronounce English words, *The Jackson 5ive*, *The Osmonds*, and of course *Top of the Pops*. *Bonanza* was the boys' favourite, I especially enjoyed *The Champions*, and *The New Avengers*; the leading actresses were beautiful, and I would sometimes copy their hairstyles and use Mum's makeup to imitate the look.

Our home was a humble one, with second-hand furniture and worn-out carpets. The house itself was constantly in need of repair and looked in a state of disarray, so although we tried to keep it tidy, it always felt cluttered. The smell of spices being cooked was never a problem back home, but became an issue especially when Dad would fry fish. Together with Mum's curry, the smell would linger for days and stayed on our clothes, which could prove embarrassing, especially when we had guests over. Thinking back, the way we lived might have been the reason why I avoided having friends over, because I was afraid of being judged or having people think less of me. After all, I was trying to fit in. Back home, Dad was such an important figure and highly regarded, but seeing how humble he had become made me dismiss my own culture as inferior to that of this country.

Although Eric was busy with work and continually studying, when necessary he could be harsh and demonstrate a certain strictness in order to keep us on track. Gert especially was becoming a handful. Like Marie, Eric was particular about hygiene, and it's safe to say they were both on the verge of obsessive behaviour when it came to keeping clean and tidy.

Eric landed himself a full-time job at a firm in the city, which he took seriously. We started to see less and less of him. He would wake early for his bath and then dress smartly for work. He had an impeccable dress sense. After a while, I noticed he became more conscious about his image, and started going out more in the evenings and at weekends. With less time on his hands, he'd offer me pocket money to shine his shoes, iron his shirt, run his bath or clean his bedroom window, which I didn't mind doing; I looked up to him, as he was hard-working and focused on a better life for himself. I watched carefully how he organised himself. At times, he would help me with my homework, especially Maths and English.

It wasn't long before he told Mum about Rose. She was distantly related to us, although I couldn't remember ever meeting her. She had four brothers, and came from a decent, respectful family. Initially when Rose and Eric went out, she had to be chaperoned by two of her brothers, Bill and John, and sometimes Marie and I would join them. The brothers were kind and generous, with old-fashioned values; they paid for everything. Our time spent with them was hilarious; we enjoyed their company and laughed a lot. They took us to the cinema, to restaurants and various bars in the West End of London. We'd also go to the monthly Mauritian dance, where families could take children as young as five to these social gatherings. There would be dancing and, of course, Mauritian snacks on sale. I enjoyed going there; it was a shame it was only once a month.

It was my first taste of social life, which I loved and wanted more of. The West End is a truly wonderful place with lots to do and see. The place really came alive at night, and the buzz and sparkling lights made it even more magical. People were smartly dressed, with young ladies made up to the nines; the West End was certainly the place to be seen, and it was important to look the part.

Although I looked forward to going there, I was never totally comfortable with the way I looked. My clothes were old-fashioned and either too big or too small. I'd never been clothes shopping. On the other hand, Gert had it all. She spent all her part-time wages on looking the part, and she had an amazing selection of modern clothes, which she'd reluctantly let me borrow. After a while, it became a habit and she started to notice clothes and makeup missing, giving her cause to lock her wardrobe. However, I came up with a plan to gain access by removing the back panel of the wardrobe to get to it: genius! I would do this on many occasions and it was a while before she realised how it was done and by whom. Understandably, she wasn't very happy about it and it caused a rift between us, which I resented her for. On reflection, I should have respected the fact that she'd worked hard for these and cared about her stuff, but being young I didn't understand what that meant at the time. I just wanted to look as good as her.

Gert left school at fifteen and went straight into work, as she was more interested in earning money to buy new clothes, makeup, and records. She'd have the latest David Cassidy hits blasting over and over again in the bedroom, which often annoyed Dad. He'd keep shouting for the volume to be turned down. Even Marie got fed up with the constant playing of music, and once threw out all the records, threatening to burn them at the bottom of the garden.

Teenage tension was starting to brew in the house and Gert began to rebel, with a few disagreements on the subject of clothes. She was hardly at home, which Dad wasn't happy about. She was an attractive young girl and she caught the eyes of many from the opposite sex, especially those at work. I once noticed her smoking, so, as you do, I too started this terrible habit, of trying to be a bit more like her. Every so often, I'd nick and hide the odd cigarette from Mum's pack; she didn't have a clue.

Dad was strict. He'd show his temper by raising his voice, and use hand gestures to indicate we'd get a slap, but I never recall him hitting any one of us. It wasn't in his character.

Gert met a local Greek lad named Evis. She was always looking for the chance to sneak out at night. When Mum became aware of this, she would try and keep the secret by letting her in at night, just to keep the peace. Marie and I got away with it, because we'd be out with Eric and Rose. Late one night, Dad found Gert sneaking back home while saying goodbye to young Evis. Dad chased him down the street with a knife, but he wanted to scare him off and teach her a lesson. After that, her focus was on leaving home to be free.

She met Gary at a printing firm where they both worked. Naturally, he was attracted to her. It wasn't long before they started dating, initially on the quiet, but soon introduced him to the family. Dad wasn't too happy at first, because of the culture difference. Ideally, he'd see us married off to good Catholic Mauritian boys. We were all keen to meet her new man. Like Gert, I too was into good looks, so I guessed he'd be attractive. I remember that when I saw him for the first time, my first impression was how similar he was to the lead singer from Sweet, with a mix of David Cassidy. He was tall – and that was without his platform shoes – slim built, with blond, shoulder-length hair, neatly parted in the middle, and he was wearing a tight-fitting shirt, tucked into a pair of light-blue bell-bottom trousers. Overall, he looked like he'd walked out of a teen magazine. I could see the attraction.

I was shy and not confident enough to speak to him, given my lack of English, not to mention he was the first English boy that had ever entered our house. He started coming round a little more often, and over a short period he'd speak to me about music whilst waiting for Gert to get ready. We talked about my favourite singers like David Essex, David Cassidy and Donny Osmond and bands like Sweet. He'd laugh and tell me that I should listen to some serious music, and he promised to bring some for me to listen to. Sure enough, the next time he brought along a David Bowie record, and a Roxy Music vinyl album called *Siren*. As I listened, he increased the volume so loud I was worried that Dad or Marie was going to tell us off. It would have been embarrassing for me, and for Gert to be told off in front of a boy.

I tried hard not to show my concerns, and simply said, 'Yes it's great. I love it!' in the hope that he'd turn it off. Deep down I wasn't keen on the sound. He left them with me and said to let him know what I thought.

Naturally, I wanted to have a conversation about it, so I forced myself to listen carefully to every track, trying to understand the meaning of the lyrics. It was really strange and so different from what I was used to. Wanting to be in the know, I'd play these every day after school, until one afternoon Dad had heard enough; he reached his limit with it all. He barged into the bedroom, scratched the needle off the record and threw the disc out of the window. Shocked, I ran out to pick it up. It wasn't mine, after all, and it worried me, to have to give it back in that condition. As it turned out, though, Gary didn't mind; he understood that Dad was strict.

# Chapter 7
# My Discovery

Roxy Music's album cover *Siren* featured the model Jerry Hall made up as a siren/mermaid. She was alluring and glamorous, and reminded me of the vision I saw as a child in the sea. Even though the record was slightly damaged, I kept wanting to play it because it was different. It grew on me after a while. I especially liked the saxophone and long instrumental pieces on various tracks. Bowie, on the other hand, appealed to me even more. He was unique. I admired his confidence, and the attitude that came with it. He didn't seem to care how he came across, which at the time separated him from other artists.

I fed off his confidence. As I read more and more about him, I wanted to be as daring as he was, in his sense of fashion and attitude towards life in general. The word 'bisexual' didn't mean anything to me, nor did it bother me. I'd imitate his singing voice, using lyrics that had deeper meanings that I was yet to understand. I became a fan in no time. Bowie helped me grow. I gained self-esteem and confidence, and he helped me realise I could be whoever I want to be and still be admired, at the time. I took myself a little too seriously in trying to fit in. I also took a liking to Marc Bolan after reading he was local and had spent time in areas that we had lived in, including Stamford Hill and Stoke Newington.

I can't say that I was rebelling, but my behaviour was different. My time was taken up experimenting with fashion and makeup, and reading pop magazines, which I bought using the pocket money Eric gave me. I especially liked *Smash Hits* and

*Mirabelle*, which had large posters in. I'd hang these on the wall, knowing it would cause arguments between Marie and me.

Before leaving school, I took part in a three-week work experience at the GPO telephone exchange at Faraday Buildings in the city. I trained as a bilingual telephonist, where my skill of the French language helped. I learnt how to operate a PMBX switchboard, which was a telephone system where calls received are connected by plugging various coloured cables into the relevant jacks. They were pleased with my work and offered me the chance of a position once I left school, which I was happy with. However, the constant use of French defeated the object of me trying to learn English. Therefore, I gave up on the idea.

Alma and I often talked about our future and what we should do about our education. She wanted to be an athlete and would continue her studies connected to sports. My lack of English limited me in more ways than one. At the time, it didn't encourage me to read; the images in magazines were the only thing that appealed to me, but I wasn't learning anything about the bigger world. I felt held back. Things needed to change.

It was clear I needed to learn English properly. I didn't just want to know words, I wanted to understand their meanings, how they should sound, be spelt and be grammatically correct, so at fifteen, I left school to focus on simply learning the language. I needed to think in English and better understand the culture in order to make something of myself. I enrolled at Stoke Newington College of Further Education to complete my CSE in English.

During my time there, I realised having English friends would be helpful. I'd carefully listen to their conversation and how the language was used. Being invited to their homes helped me understand their way of life, including the food they ate, which was generally meat and two veg. The contrast to our culture was huge. It was always interesting listening to their chitchat about life in general. Their behaviour was shocking at times. They'd teach me swear words, which left them laughing, because my accent didn't suit it. I never felt comfortable using those words as such. However, I took note of the way swearing was used, with the intonation, and impact it had between sentences. I didn't like hearing foul language, especially when used by girls, maybe because of the way I was brought up. The constant use of swear words made that person sound uneducated somehow, as though they were limited with their own knowledge of words. On the subject of socialising and drinking, it amazed some to hear that I'd never been to a pub, or drunk alcohol for that matter. I completed my exams, although not brilliantly, but passed to an acceptable level, armed with a better understanding of the language would give me some confidence to move forward.

Marie and I went to a Mauritian social gathering in Leicester Square. It was surely a small world when I saw Monsieur Marcel who happened to be the main organiser at the club. We went over to say hi. He was surprised to see how much we'd grown, and made it a point to introduce us to a few people, including a Mauritian girl named Henriette. She was full of life, and seemed to know everything and everyone. We clicked right away. She lived in North London and we arranged to meet up, which we did now and then for a few months. She became aware that we weren't well off as a family and knew that I was broke.

One afternoon she invited me to meet her older sister Amélie, who lived in Holloway. My first impression when she opened the door was *Wow!* In her early twenties, she was beautiful and looked like a model. I wondered whether she might have even been a dancer, as she had a certain look.

Her flat was small and dimly lit, with a red silk scarf draped over a lampshade. It was afternoon, but all the curtains were drawn. Soft Motown music was playing in the background, and what you could see looked untidy, with clothes strewn across the bed and some scattered over pieces of furniture. I couldn't help noticing there were lots of banknotes left out on the dressing table, along with makeup, and perfume bottles.

Amélie talked to us from her dressing table. At times I'd catch her sizing me up, before telling me how beautiful I was, with the potential to be a model. I timidly smiled and disagreed with her, her confidence making me nervous. Henriette seemed to look up to her and was in awe of her presence.

Amélie suggested that I could make money with my looks, grabbing a few notes from her dressing table, waving it in the air, and saying, 'This here is easy money. If you're interested, come and see how I make it.'

It seemed obvious, she wanted to impress me by pointing at the gifts and clothes she'd received, with talk of places that she had visited in her line of work. It didn't take much to convince me. It got me all excited, so I agreed, and arranged to meet Henriette in a bar at St Pancras one afternoon. Amélie sat a distance from us, but still in view, dressed as though she was going on a night out, with full makeup. Not knowing what to expect, I kept insisting that we should at least say hello, but Henriette said it wasn't possible, and that I should just watch to see how she works. We sat there sipping on Coke, patiently waiting for something to happen.

Shortly after, an older gentleman in his fifties approached and casually greeted her with a kiss on both cheeks. I asked who he was, and whether we should go and say hi. Henriette giggled. I watched them both as they left together. I was confused at what I had just seen, Henriette explained it all to me, suggesting that I could make, what she called 'easy money'. Being a good Catholic girl, I thought it was immoral, and didn't like the sound of what she was involved in. Nowadays, I would argue that the act was no more than two consenting adults simply 'hooking up'. The only difference is being paid for the service she provides which may not be acceptable by some. I see it as brave and dangerous work, which is why I would not want to do it.

Alma couldn't believe it when I told her about my recent experience with Amélie, and what they were trying to get me involved in. Of course, I didn't have a clue about the birds and the bees. Alma explained enough to make me realise that I should keep away from these people and concentrate on finding a good job. For a young person, she made a lot of sense, which I admired about her. She opened my eyes to a lot of stuff I was totally oblivious to. It was clear that I'd led a sheltered life, and was naive when it came to the opposite sex. Mum didn't even explain what a period was. We were reserved as a family. It didn't seem appropriate to talk about relationships, nor was it a subject that was ever discussed between us sisters. We were none the wiser, and I think we were just expected to learn along the way.

Henriette realised I was trying to avoid her and tried everything to get me to see her sister again. Eventually, I told her that I had found a job and was busy doing other things. Even though I had reservations about the job offer at the GPO, which also meant working nights and weekends, I took it on anyway. I worked there for eight months, but although enjoyable, the constant use of French was - as I thought - really affecting my English and impacted me socially. I decided to find another job that suited my needs and would help me use the language, which could only mean working with the public. After my search, I managed to find a full-time job closer to home, working as a cashier at Tempo Electrical Retail in Dalston, where I'd learn to deal with money and customers. The help I got from Eric came in useful with this.

Eric and Gert were great dancers, mainly to northern soul and funk music. They were known to have won trophies after taking part in dance competitions. I vividly recall the night a group of us had gone to the famous Mecca Dance Hall in Leicester Square to watch them dance. It was truly amazing. They won first prize and were given a trophy as a dancing duo. It was like a scene from *Saturday Night Fever* and a truly proud moment. We left there in the early hours. With no public transport and not enough money for a taxi, we walked back to East London, arriving at three in the morning. It was freezing, but I had become accustomed to the cold, and being young didn't seem to affect us somehow.

In 1974, Eric was spending more and more time with Rose, and stayed over some evenings as their relationship was becoming serious. Unsurprisingly, he proposed to her. We were all thrilled for them and were excited about the forthcoming wedding. Eric's absence allowed the younger ones to run riot. The situation was out of control, which was reflected in the interior of the house. There were big dents and holes on the staircase, and the wooden flooring and other parts of the house showed signs of wear and tear.

Doors and windows were being left wide open. I guess in those days it felt safe to do so, and we didn't see the dangers lurking until we were broken into. Coming downstairs one morning, Mum noticed our meter on the wall had been broken into and emptied. Not so long after, we had another break-in when a tall, young man entered the house through Mum and Dad's bedroom window, which was easily accessible from the nearby steps below. Dad heard a noise and found him, literally standing over them.

Dad jumped out of bed and shouted, 'Get the gun!' at which the man jumped out of the window, never to return. Of course, there was no gun in the house, but Dad's voice must have been very convincing.

In the summer of that year, Eric left home after his marriage to Rose.

I started adjusting to the English way of life. Although the climate and culture difference proved challenging at times, fish and chips became a favoured choice. The doors were constantly revolving with changes in our lives. Alma, whom I can safely say was a true friend, had moved to south-east London, but we would often write to each other. Although I never saw Amélie again, I remained friends with Henriette because she was fun to be around, but you couldn't really trust her. I always got the feeling she had an agenda, but she was the only friend close by. When we could afford to, we'd go to various dance halls in north London, like The Lyceum, Tottenham Royal, which was impressive (it had a revolving stage with lots of plastic palm trees dotted around, adding a beach party feel to the place), and Charlie Brown's. By then, as well as pop and rock, I enjoyed reggae, soul and funk music. Life felt good. I was enjoying myself, and my confidence grew, along with a sense of self-esteem. My spark gave me a zest for life itself and nothing was going to spoil the fun.

At seventeen, I evolved in so many ways and realised it was cool not to fit in. Now earning a wage, I could afford to change the way I looked, and my fashion sense was the first thing that needed addressing. Influenced by Marc Bolan, the 70s rock chic style appealed to me. My skinny figure helped complete the look, wearing sparkly halter-neck tops, hot pants and mini dresses in the summer. My choice of disco outfits would be more glamorous, with white flared trousers, Lycra and bright red satin leggings, not to mention the dreaded platforms. It's a wonder I didn't break my neck back then. The second glances I got from the opposite sex were unusual, but they made me feel good.

Female models in magazines were wearing trouser suits and it was a daring look, but soon became more acceptable. I remember my first ever visit to a hairdressing salon and being given a young male hairdresser to style my hair. His name was Les and he had that Bowie look about him: a little on the effeminate side, tall, good looking and strangely but trendily dressed in baggy gangster-like clothing. Like Bowie, he wore it with confidence. Realising I was shy, he tried to make me feel comfortable by making small talk. I told him that I liked the Purdy look from *The New Avengers*, which he agreed would look great. Whilst getting my first bob hairstyle, I was flicking through a fashion magazine.

Les pointed his comb at a flared white trouser suit worn by Twiggy and said, 'I can see you in that; you look like her.'

Having a complex about being thin made me wonder whether his comment was flattering or not, but she was one of the models I admired, so I took it as my first ever compliment from a male, which boosted my confidence. I and my sisters loved my new hairdo.

At seventeen, Gert was desperate to leave and have a place of her own. She moved in with Gary's parents until they married in 1975. They later rented a flat in Wapping in a large warehouse that had been converted. It ran parallel to the northern bank of the Thames. Her new life was about to begin and she'd face reality.

I, too, would soon have my eyes opened. After a few trips to the hairdressers, Les decided to ask me out. Shocked, I said I'd let him know. That evening I couldn't stop thinking about him. I was excited at the thought, and nervous about a first date. How to tell Mum and Dad played on my mind all night. Our home was in a state of disarray and didn't want Les to see how we lived. I'm sure my older siblings felt the same way. I was embarrassed to have my friends round, let alone a boy that I fancied.

I agreed to meet him. At first glance, he looked like he'd walked out of *Vogue* magazine, confidently wearing an off-white double-breasted suit with dark braces, a silk scarf around his neck and two-tone black and white brogues on his feet, completing the look with his short, feathered hairstyle. I was in the company of my first ever boyfriend. It felt good and real. He was attentive and made me feel comfortable. We laughed and joked as we walked around the West End. I felt as though he was showing me off, but I noticed people staring and gazing at him. He looked different. Girls would flirtatiously giggle as they walked past us, but none of it fazed him. It was as though he was used to it. We ended up at a nightclub called La Poubelle, and the place was buzzing with the beat of soul and funk music. He was a familiar face, especially with the ladies, and he knew how to strut his stuff on the dance floor. I was on cloud nine and loved every minute of my first date.

Unbeknown to Mum and Dad, I would meet him regularly. Apart from my friend Alma, no one else knew I was seeing someone, even though the relationship was platonic. Nothing intimate had happened, not even a proper kiss. We were just good friends who enjoyed each other's company. On one occasion Les took me shopping, as he thought my clothing was a bit hippyish and he wanted me to fit in with him. I opted for a trouser suit, which was all the rage at the time. Being a size 6 and trying these on in the changing room made me look like Bowie. I bought it anyway.

On Valentine's Day 1976, Les invited me to his place, as his parents were away for the weekend. I felt a bit nervous, as it was the first time I'd be alone with him somewhere more personal. He prepared a prawn cocktail for starters with a club sandwich. I thought it was sweet of him. Afterwards he showed me old pictures of himself and his family. As usual, we laughed and giggled about my accent and bad English, which he corrected every so often. Then came a knock at the door. I remained in the lounge, but could hear a female raising her voice on the doorstep. I got up to see what the commotion was, and there in the entrance stood a young foreign-looking girl, shouting and threatening Les. She was crying as he slammed the door on her. He walked me back into the lounge to explain that she was an ex who couldn't let go.

Our evening was ruined. Was this a love triangle situation I read about in magazines? One thing for sure, I didn't like it! I asked if he could walk me home. After a short distance, the same girl appeared, together with a few others who had waited around the corner in ambush, shouting at both of us, calling me every name under the sun. I felt under attack. Why were they angry at me? I tried to calm the situation, using my limited English to explain we were just friends, but they weren't having any of it. She was making it sound as though they were still together, which upset me a little, so I told them both they should sort it out, as I was out of the picture. I simply walked away and didn't look back.

Had I insisted on staying put, it could have ended differently. I hated confrontation. Not only was it an embarrassing situation, but I also felt deceived and disappointed, which left a strange feeling in the pit of my stomach, one that I had never experienced before. My pride wasn't going to allow me to be ridiculed. I can't say I was broken-hearted as I don't think I was in love with him, just sad to lose a friend like him.

# Chapter 8
# The Trap

You could safely say I was very shy prior to meeting Les. Like most, I wasn't comfortable being stared at. In fact, I hated it. I was constantly preoccupied with how people judged my appearance, given my skinny body that was always dressed in tatty, ill-fitting hand-me-down clothing. This habit has stayed with me to this day. I walk with my head down, usually gazing on the ground to avoid catching people's glances. Back then, when I felt I was being stared at, I believed they were studying my imperfection. Hearing the constant calls of a wolf whistle taught me that men were checking me out! I can't lie, it felt good, but I was always wary of their intention.

After that dreadful Valentine's evening with Les, although he continued to cut my hair, socially, I distanced myself from him. However, I missed having him as a friend. My time with him was invaluable. He helped me to appreciate and love myself. I must have been easily influenced, because Gary was able to add an alternative sound to my choice of music, and Les had opened my eyes to the fashion world. This new confidence made me comfortable in my own skin. With my growing self-esteem, I started to appreciate who I was as a person. All my spare money was then spent on the latest fashion and makeup. Evenings out with friends became more enjoyable. I was happy. Life was good and I was going to embrace it to the full.

For a good chunk of my teenage life, I dreamt of being in the limelight, perhaps to feature in fashion magazines or become a dancer like those on *Top of the Pops*. Although I loved singing, I really didn't have the power behind my voice to 'make it', but my new approach and positiveness helped keep the dream alive. At seventeen, I was no Jerry Hall, but more Twiggy with boobs. Gerry was a friend of a friend who had done some modelling himself. He once suggested that I had potential, and should consider a career in this field. Being 5ft 4" didn't cut it for a catwalk model; facially, maybe. I agreed, to go with him to his agency in Old Bond Street.

Nervous but excited at the same time, I felt unprepared, and didn't know what to expect. Gerry had informed the agency in advance about my arrival, so the young pretty receptionist was expecting us, Gerry waited outside as he didn't want to come in with me. I was instructed to sit in the waiting area, as she dialled an extension to announce my arrival. Within minutes, she was leading me towards a highly polished door, knocking before entering a large, dark office, thick with the unmistakable smell of old cigarettes, and very masculine in the way it was furnished. Before leaving, she introduced me to the man slumped in a red-leather swivel chair, pulling himself closer to his desk.

He used the fingers on one hand to beckon me to come closer.

'Ah, come in.'

As I walked towards him, I could see him pressing shredded tobacco into his pipe. We weren't alone. Two other middle-aged men dressed in suits stood by the large desk that took up most of the space in the middle, surrounded by large chesterfield leather armchairs.

My focus was on the man behind the desk who was doing all the talking. I assumed he was in charge. He looked me up and down for a few seconds, before inviting me to sit opposite. His stare didn't exactly make me feel comfortable. He asked me for my portfolio, but I didn't know what that meant, but replied, 'I don't have it,' I said.

He laughed out loud, throwing his head backwards.

Once he'd repositioned himself, he said, 'You can't come in here without a portfolio – but never mind that. What experience have you got in the field of modelling?'

'None.'

He shook his head to express his time was being wasted. I naively sat there feeling stupid and pathetic!

Then I innocently said, 'I'm interested in face modelling,' thinking my look was all it took.

He looked up at the two men, as if they could read his mind. One of them suggested I should remove my blouse.   I thought it was odd, and questioned why. He commented on my jet-black hair, which would be ideal for a shoot they had in mind, and wanted to see my neckline. So, I stupidly, slowly and reluctantly, undid my blouse. He asked me to stand up, and lift my skirt further, to see my thighs. My instincts were screaming at me, *don't do it!* as it didn't feel right. As they all glared at me, I stood there, feeling bare and cheap.

I quickly straightened myself, and pulled my blouse shut, and said, 'It's my face that I hope you'd be interested in.'

It was clear they weren't interested in my face. I just wanted to leave the room. They were trying to convince me to stay, making it look like they were trying to help me.

One of them added, 'You could be a topless model.'

Although I didn't fully understand what it entailed, it just didn't sound right. I quickly gathered myself, apologised and left the room. Even saying sorry didn't feel right. I was clueless.

One of the men walked me out of the room, and with a reassuring tone said, 'Look, I'm a professional photographer. I'm sorry you had to go through that. Sorry if you felt uncomfortable.'

I didn't respond, but kept my head low in disgust. He proceeded to reassure me that I had potential in the beauty business, and asked whether I'd allow him to take my pictures at his studio. His words went over my head. I just wanted to leave the building, He gave me his business card, which I took, just to

76

cut him short. He further suggested I could bring a chaperone along if it helped. I felt sick with shame, and thought, *if my family could see me, what would they think?* I was angry with myself for being so naive, and vowed never to put myself in that position again. So, my dreams of ever being a model were shattered!

From my disappointed glance towards Gerry, who by now was sitting in the waiting area, it was obvious that things hadn't gone well. He spoke to the photographer, who seemed familiar with him. After all was explained he couldn't believe what had happened, but tried to convince me that the photographer was for real, and that I could trust him, as he was professional and good at what he does, and I should not dismiss him. I didn't want to hear any more about it.

The experience opened my eyes to the ugliness out there. In a way, incidents like this and Henriette's sister thinking I could be a high-class call girl helped me be realistic about my future. I carried on living the simple, but safer way of life. Working at Tempo was okay, but I needed a change.

One afternoon, Dad and I were buying cheap fruit and vegetables on Ridley Road Market in Dalston. I noticed an advert in the window of a small unit, it stated 'Telephonist Wanted – Apply Within.' Dad waited for me as I went up some flights of stairs that led to a small workshop. Standing there was a young man fixing a radio monitor. For a minute he stared at me in wonder. I told him I was enquiring about the position advertised in the window.

I thought I'd impress him, and questioned, 'Is the system a PABX or PMBX?'

He gazed at me for a moment, and in a heavy cockney accent, replied, 'It's a bladdy phone, innit! Can you use it?'

All embarrassed, I said, 'Of course!'

That very moment, the phone rang, and he said, 'Do you wanna answer that?', which I did.

He then added, 'You can start on Monday at 9 sharp!'

There was no discussion of wages or experience of any sort. As I left, I found myself bewildered at what had just happened. I can't explain it, but his tone made me feel nervous that he was one you shouldn't mess with.

Excited at the prospect of a new job, I instantly handed my notice in at Tempo, and started my new job the Monday after. As I entered the workshop, he introduced himself properly as Alan Sugar. He explained about his new distribution centre in Garman Road and what the company Amstrad stood for. He made a joke about the flared trousers I was wearing.

'You could sweep Ridley Road market up with those.'

He didn't mince his words, and would tell you exactly what he thought. Asking me what I enjoyed, I told him I liked fashion and music. He asked, what I was into.

'I'm a big fan of Bowie and Marc Bolan,' I said.

He chuckled and said, 'Bolan? I went to school with him.'

My eyes lit up and I thought *Bonus!* The reception at the new premises was large and modern. I realised that I must have impressed him with my earlier question; as it turned out, the switchboard I was operating, was a PABX system. I enjoyed working there and quickly settled into my new role. Everyone seemed friendly, even Alan. Although scary at times, he did on occasion demonstrate a gentle side.

I took on a Saturday job at Biba's busy store in Kensington, working on the makeup counter. Although hard at times, it was fun and hip! Many of the customers were stylish and beautiful to look at. After work, some of the girls would invite me to join them at a bar or club of some sort. One evening I was invited to a twenty-first birthday celebration. On arrival, we had to go down a steep staircase, which led to a wine cellar where the private party was being held. As I reached the bottom, greeting us was the birthday girl, the most beautiful girl I had ever set eyes on. She looked foreign, with long shiny black hair, and the biggest blue eyes! I couldn't help noticing the gold chain she wore, which had an Arabic font inscription of some sort. I commented on its beauty, as I thought it was unusual, I asked what it meant.

She mumbled a strange name, and said, 'But you can call me Zoyla.'

The name stuck with me for many years. I even wanted to change my own to that of hers, as it suited her beauty.

One evening at a house party, a friend introduced me to a Mauritian chap. His name was Pat and he wasn't bad looking. He had that certain John Travolta look about him, with the most amazing green eyes, but more importantly he was pleasant to talk to. The evening saw us playing a game of cat and mouse on the stairs, playing it cool. I felt we were both keen. We agreed to meet again. It starts with that butterfly feeling in the pit of your stomach. I can't explain why, but it felt different, as I looked forward to seeing him again and again. We dated for a while before he wanted to meet the family. Feeling a little embarrassed about the home I lived in, I kept putting it off, at the same time explaining that Dad was very strict.

He introduced me to his family, who seemed kind, and friendly. He lived with his mum, together with his auntie, her husband and his cousins. There were at least seven adults in total living in a big house. Their interest in wanting to know more about my family and our background indicated that they might have approved of me. Two months after, the time was right to tell Mum about him. She seemed pleased that he was Catholic and of the same culture. I'd let her break the news to Dad, who then wanted to meet him. We arranged for this to take place at Dad's work. Naturally, I was nervous. He was the first man I ever introduced to the family. The meeting went well, all things considered. Dad's invitation for him and his family to join us for dinner was enough to confirm he was happy about our courtship, after which things moved really fast. It wasn't long before they came to dinner. I prayed they wouldn't judge us by the state the house was in.

Pat became aware of my dreams of becoming a model, and of course, I told him of the terrible experience I had, but he encouraged me to not give up. He said I should still pursue it and contact the photographer. I thought about it long and hard, but knowing this time round someone would be with me helped with the decision to contact the studio.

A photoshoot for facial modelling was arranged. On arrival, there were several people in the studio, which included a makeup artist, stylist and so on. I introduced Pat as my boyfriend. The photographer seemed happy to have him there, and explained all that would take place during the shoot. Furthermore, I could have some of these to start a portfolio. Having agreed to all of that, the shoot began.

It was going well and the photographer was doing a great job. Everyone involved worked professionally. In fact, they made me feel special and comfortable, with no inappropriate behaviour. As explained, he would need to have my neckline exposed to achieve the look they were after, which involved wrapping bottle-green crepe paper over my own clothing, and around my top half, for a contrast. Halfway through the shoot, for some reason, Pat didn't seem happy. He came over and grabbed me by the hands and said we should finish, and pulled me away from the set to talk to me. I was shocked and embarrassed. I tried to reason with him, but he wasn't having any of it.

He simply said, 'I don't like him touching you!', which surely he would have had to do to get it right.

I insisted that the photographer was not acting inappropriately in any way. The shoot had to be stopped and the photographer suggested we call it a day. I felt terrible and didn't know how I could ever come back to it.

The combination of being young, naive and having led a sheltered life didn't prepare me for what to expect in a loving relationship. I thought what I had with Pat was true romance, based on him doting on me and telling me how beautiful and special I was. I thought he was trying to protect me from the dangers lurking, which made me love him even more. He wouldn't let me out of sight if he had the chance, but in reality, he didn't want anyone else to have me. I was his and no one else's. I allowed him to make decisions for me, which gave him control over me. Back then, my only defence was my instincts, which I rarely listened to. Whatever the reasons, life did not prepare me to read the signs and how to deal with them.

The bells should have been ringing after the episode at the studio, and hearing little comments like, 'Who cut your hair?' 'Why did you choose to wear that dress tonight?' Then he'd lose his mind when he found out that Les was the one that cut my hair. He hadn't met Les, but he was envious of him. He'd even lose his mind when other men looked my way; it didn't matter if I avoided anyone's glance. There were constant questions about people I worked with. He'd want to meet me after work just to see the set-up and who my work colleagues were.

One evening, I wore my favourite off-the-shoulder satin dress. True enough, I was attracting attention from other men. Even women admired the way I was dressed, but this did not sit well with him. He thought the dress was too revealing, and purposely spilt his drink all over it. There were many evenings out like these, where the night would be cut short and I'd have to go home earlier than usual.

At the time, I ignored the signs, but it was pure jealousy. I didn't see it as a crime or something I should worry about. Maybe I liked the fact that he was a little jealous. It made me feel special, but it was soon apparent that the attention I was getting from other men bothered him. So, to avoid a scene or an argument, I behaved differently around him. I wore less makeup, I'd dress to please him, I'd look away from those glaring at me. I started to lose my spark. Even my friends remarked how my mood had changed. Pat made sure I saw less and less of them, and wanted me all to himself.

We had been dating for about six months when, without notice, Pat came round one evening and spoke to Dad alone. I didn't think anything of it. After a little while, he appeared in the dining room where I was sat, and on one knee, he took out a ring from a box, and proposed. I was stunned! I looked at him as if to say, *what are you thinking?* He said he had already asked Dad for my hand in marriage. I was in shock! I went into the other room where Mum and Dad were chatting.

I asked, 'What happened?'

I noticed that Dad had tears in his eyes, I'd never seen him cry before this day. He looked up at me and said, 'I thought that's what you wanted.'

I shouted 'No!' and went back into the dining room.

Pat was sitting holding the ring still and begged! 'Please say yes.'

I looked at him and felt trapped. I didn't know what to say or do. It was an ugly antique ruby ring that looked like it had been worn before. I hated it, but he kept insisting, so although my instincts were telling me it was wrong, I took the ring, and tried it on, thinking, *let's give him the benefit of doubt.* I knew I liked being around him and confused these feelings as love. I truly didn't know what real love was.

Pat was a typical Gemini; at times he'd show his nice side. He surprised me with tickets to a Bowie concert; it was The Thin White Duke Tour. All of Bowie's brilliance came together when he entered the stage. The fans went berserk, as I did. I couldn't sit still. I was on my feet the whole way through, hearing songs that I knew the lyrics to. Although I wanted to express my passion for him, I controlled how much I gave off, but he knew he couldn't compete with the feelings I had for Bowie, I guess that's what made him so jealous. When the song 'Heroes' was being performed, I was mesmerised; I imagined he was singing directly at me; I truly wanted to be his queen. The lyrics to 'Rebel Rebel' encapsulated just what I once felt as a rebel teenager. Halfway through, I turned around to look at Pat. He was sitting slouched in his seat with his eyes closed! I couldn't believe that he could ignore all the noise and magic going on in the room, and he looked pathetic. It was an enjoyable day that was hard to forget. If only he had shared my passion.

Soon after, the family was on the move. We'd been offered a large five-bedroom house in Northampton. New housing developments and businesses were being built to accommodate the influx of overpopulation in London. Dad had always commented that London was not an ideal place to bring up a family. He missed living in the countryside, so, he jumped at the chance, happy to move to such an area.

We had two or three months before we were to marry. Together with my job, it was agreed that I'd stay behind and live with Pat's family until we found a place of our own. Although Marie had also met a young Mauritian man named Jim, they too planned to marry, but she decided to move with the family to Northampton until her wedding day. In hindsight, I wished I had done the same. It might have given me more time to think about what I was about to get myself into; but I guess that's how life teaches us, from our mistakes.

# Chapter 9
# Disastrous Beginnings

After moving in with Pat's family, we saved hard for a place of our own. I chose to sleep alone until my wedding day. The toilet set up was outside; definitely not ideal, especially in bad weather, or if you're desperate. There were many house rules, which I respected, and I would help do my bit around the house. The family had a habit of locking doors and would encourage saving electricity at every opportunity, which was reasonable. However, I would forget this rule and be pulled up so many times for having the lights on too long. Although some of the rules were a bit harsh, I put up with them, knowing they were helping us finance the wedding arrangements, which was decent of them. They organised everything, from choosing my dress to the caterers. They even organised my hen do, which was sitting in his auntie's flat, sharing a bottle of wine with his cousin.

My wedding day came on a cold January in 1977. I had just turned nineteen; it should have been the happiest day of my life. Instead, sitting at my dressing table, sipping on a hot cup of tea, I felt miserable. Once again, my instincts were failing me. Although they were telling me not to go through with it, I worried about being judged harshly and what everyone else would say. After all, a lot of money had gone into organising the big day. I put all my negative thoughts down to nerves.

You name it, everything that could have possibly gone wrong on the day, did, starting with the hairdresser. Pat's mum had paid for my hair to be styled, but the salon was full of the blue rinse brigade. I left there looking twenty years older. I didn't look like me and I had to wash my hair again and blow dry it to my taste, which didn't please her in the least, but she remained calm.

Four of my sisters were bridesmaids and brother Peter was the page boy, and they had all arrived at the house to get ready. By now we were rushing and I didn't even have time to think about what I was getting myself into. Even when Dad and I travelled in the hired white 1973/74 Rolls Royce to the church, it didn't dawn on me that I was about to make the biggest mistake of my life. Once out of the car, my sisters helped straighten my dress and veil in place, before walking up the steps to the entrance of the church, but Peter accidentally stepped on my long-laced veil, which left a great big tear in it.

We were greeted at the entrance by the priest who was to marry us. Acting fidgety, he informed us that the groom had not yet arrived and proceeded to give us more bad news: the organ was not in working order and there would be no music as I walked up the aisle. I looked at Dad and started to cry, not because Pat was late or because of the lack of processional music, but because I desperately wanted him to rescue me and tell me it was okay to not go through with it. Instead, he gave me a comforting smile. If these occurrences weren't bad omens, I don't know what is.

As it turned out, Pat's car broke down on the way to church, so he and his best man had to walk, making them late by twenty minutes. They walked past us as they entered the church. Had Mum been standing with us, she would have told me that it was bad luck if the groom saw you before you get married on the day. Shaking, with tears running down my face as Dad walked me up the long aisle, I was conscious the guests would pick up on how unhappy I was. The fake smile on my face was the only emotion I shared. I tried to avoid people's glances, and the deadly silence made it feel more like a funeral. I can honestly say I can't remember any of what happened after I walked up the aisle, apart from not wanting to be there. After the ceremony, our

85

wedding car deserted us and we had to cross a busy main road to make our way to the hall opposite.

Maybe I read too many magazines or watched too many films, but I imagined that I would be surprised and whisked off to some romantic location for our honeymoon. Unfortunately, this did not happen for me. Instead, I found myself back home. It was cold with no heating on; I can't tell you how disappointed I was. I was dying to use the toilet, only to find the back door locked. So, still in my wedding dress, I stood there and weed myself, like I'd stopped caring.

Some intelligent person decided to lock all the doors in the house and take the keys with them to the wedding reception, which of course, meant we couldn't access the bedroom either. Whilst we waited for their return, Pat drank champagne, as I watched. We decided to open some of the presents that had been taken back to the house. It was around 1am when the in-laws strolled in. It truly wasn't a good start to the marriage. However, the nightmare was just beginning. Still a virgin, it was to be our first night spent together. Drunk and slumped in a chair, Pat was out for the count. So, I slept alone and silently cried, reflecting on the day's disaster.

Pat will tell you he loved me and I believe he did. My life wasn't my own, even though the control started way before we got married. Unfortunately for me, I didn't read the signs until much too late. Within weeks of being married, I started to notice the change in his family's behaviour towards me. They stopped including me in conversations. Feeling I'd overstayed my welcome, I felt uncomfortable around them. My mother-in-law enjoyed reading photo-romans (romantic French magazines), which she'd pass on to me. These taught me a lot about people's relationships and feelings of true love, which was far from my own reality. I was truly unhappy. I missed my chaotic family life on Amhurst Road. I couldn't speak to anyone about how I was feeling. I suppose I didn't want to be judged a failure.

We tried for a family straight away, which I thought was the thing to do. I was never told about birth control. Despite trying, I couldn't fall pregnant, and this was to become more of an issue with his family. Six months had passed, and his family were doubting my ability to conceive, and questions were being asked as to why I was still not with child. I felt pressured and at times made to feel unwomanly. They suggested I have tests done, as there may be something wrong with me, which I did, but doctors couldn't find a reason why it just didn't happen. At the time, no questions were being asked of Pat's capability!

Married life was not turning out the way I thought it would. It didn't help to live with his family, but that didn't matter to him as he was very close to his mum. I kept insisting that we find a place of our own. Arguments between us were on the increase. I felt trapped. Apart from going out to work, I hardly left the house. Pat stopped making me feel special, because he had me where he wanted me, under the watchful eye of his family when he wasn't around. We hardly went out. I missed seeing my friends Alma and Henriette, whom I wasn't allowed to see anymore.

One evening, after an argument, I'd had enough. I stormed out after packing a few personal belongings without planning it. I literally walked out of the house. I had no idea of where I was going. Although I can't remember what the argument was about, I'm certain it would have had something to do with his family. Pat chased me down the street, and we stood and talked, but I was adamant I didn't want to go back to the house. He tried to convince me of his undying love and that he would do anything for us to be together. He suggested going to stay at another auntie's place until we sorted ourselves out. Reluctantly, I agreed. Life there wasn't that much different, but a bit more bearable.

Gert and Gary were still living in a Tower Hamlets flat in Wapping. She was able to help Marie and Jim find a place there after they were married. I too jumped on the bandwagon and applied for a flat in the same block. Although it was a bedsit with no bathroom, I didn't mind, as it meant we were able to live our lives as a couple and start afresh.

Like everything else, it started okay. We enjoyed being alone and we had a few laughs in trying to build a life together. I couldn't cook for the life of me. The first dinner invite was to Mum and Dad. I wanted it to be perfect. I was nervous, but excited to see them. I attempted to make a chicken curry, which was ruined; I didn't use the right spices and the rice was overdone. Mum, bless her heart, threw everything out and looked through the kitchen cupboards, where she found enough ingredients to teach me how to prepare a simple dish. She was amazing like that. Mum had the knack of creating something out of nothing. I loved the idea of having people around, and I wanted it to be a regular thing. I missed seeing people.

Even though I didn't go out much, I did meet up with Gert on a couple of occasions. It was her twenty-first birthday when we met at Whitechapel railway station. The evening started with us being girly and looking forward to a nice evening out, I still remember how much we laughed. We took a silly picture in the station's photo booth, before ending up at a trendy bar. After an hour or so, I felt faint and collapsed. Gert helped a man take me out for some fresh air. In those days, I didn't eat much. I was always weak and I wasn't used to drinking back then – I guess it wasn't a good idea on an empty stomach – so the evening was cut short.

Nine months later, we moved to a one-bedroom flat in Rotherhithe, south-east London. It wasn't a lot bigger, but it had a bathroom. However, all was about to change. I sensed a shift in atmosphere as Pat's behaviour became more controlling. He had a thing about cleanliness and everything had its place. At the time, I didn't know the name or condition, but I later found out it was a case of OCD. If I didn't get things right, sarcastic remarks were used. I was made to look stupid and pathetic. He'd always apologise and laugh it off. At first, I would giggle at my clumsiness, too, and found myself taking the blame, but after a time it wore thin with me. It seemed he enjoyed belittling me.

Again, I didn't identify it as emotional abuse, because we were still able to laugh. There were fun moments, which I chose to focus on. It made up for his controlling behaviour. However, in reality, he was chipping away at my self-esteem. At first, there were no marks or bruises, but it changed me. I became introverted. Even though we were living away from his family, things between us didn't improve. I wasn't being myself, and I felt low and depressed.

Pat's jealousy became an issue. He was jealous of the admiration I had for any of my favourite actors or singers. I'll never forget the time David Bowie was a guest on Capital Radio. He was to answer questions from fans calling in. Pat even helped me make the call. I was so excited at the idea of actually having a conversation with my idol. The line was constantly engaged, but I didn't give up. Eventually it rang. I was so nervous, thinking about what to say, the DJ asked for my name, and Bowie's voice melted me, with a simple 'Hi.' The next thing I knew, the line was cut off. I looked up at Pat, who was laughing. Although I didn't see him disconnect the line, I'm almost certain it was deliberate. Why would he laugh if he didn't know what had happened? Because he couldn't stop laughing, I truly believed to this day that he had planned it that way all along, but I had no proof.

The mental abuse wasn't enough. It shifted to a slap on the face to get me to say what he wanted me to say. He would just want to hear me tell him that I was doing something that I shouldn't have done. If I disagreed with anything or he didn't hear what he wanted to hear, another slap would follow for answering back, if only to silence me. I would often be thrown on the floor and end up in a crouched position, where it would be easy to kick and punch. Over the months, the physical abuse got worse. The threats to kill were becoming more convincing and I had real fears for my life.

After a while, I found I was spending more and more time alone in the evenings, which at first meant peace. He'd stroll in, sometimes drunk, in the early hours. I hated moments like these, as it fuelled many of the arguments we had, which mostly resulted in me being hurt both physically and mentally. He had lost his job, but was spending money on new clothes, aftershave and going out with his friends. He cared more and more about his appearance. At times, he'd be gone for the whole day and all night.

Naturally, this behaviour was getting to me. My inquisitive side kicked in, and I needed to understand what was happening. I'd had enough of being silenced. I knew he wasn't being truthful. I couldn't understand how he could afford the lifestyle he was leading. Details of a tax rebate appeared on my payslip, which I know I didn't receive. After making an enquiry, it transpired that a cheque had been sent to me. It dawned on me that Pat may have forged my signature and cashed it, which would explain his recent indulgence. Although I didn't have any proof, for once my instincts allowed me to be blunt, so I confronted him. He denied it. I then threatened to report him, which by now he knew I was capable of, so he later admitted to doing it, and agreed to give me the money back when he started work. Fortunately for me, he kept his promise.

From then on, I used the time I had to become resourceful. I refused to be silent and be made a fool of. I questioned everything and would often confront him about things that I suspected. I had my suspicions that he was having an affair, which would give me enough reason to leave and divorce him. Marriage in our culture was taken seriously. It would be scandalous to file for divorce. Women were often made to feel inferior for failing to have children and stand by their husbands, or at least that's what I was led to believe. As a child, having seen Stella and Fanfan's turbulent relationship made me accept my own as just the way marriage is.

Over the months, I tried to find the answers by going through his pockets and smelling his clothes after he'd been out for the night, the usual behaviour if you had suspicions about a partner. I didn't trust him, but I had no proof. There was a time when I had just come out of the hospital, after having had surgery for a gynae procedure, still with stitches in a wound that hadn't healed properly. While alone one evening, I wandered around the flat searching for answers. Hidden in an airing cupboard, I found a cine camera with reels and reels of film, and lots of what I now know to be hardcore porn magazines. Holding the film strips up to the light, I could see the negatives of what appeared to be people in sex positions, but I couldn't be sure. My upbringing didn't teach me about such things and I had never seen a porn magazine before that day. Looking through the pages, I felt disgusted at the thought that he would rather look at these instead of me, so in my anger I destroyed the films and tore the magazines to shreds, which I purposely left on the floor of the entrance so he would see them when he came in.

I knew this meant trouble and braced myself for what could potentially have a terrible ending, but I felt better for doing it. I had arrived at a stage in my life, where I didn't care what happened to me. After all, if it was all innocent, why hide it? I sat in the bath soaking myself. I could hear the key in the door. He walked in, I heard shuffling in the corridor, then total silence. My mind was racing with thoughts of how I was going to survive any beatings. At that, he burst through into the bathroom, grabbed hold of me, shouting, followed by slaps, asking why I'd done what I did, suggesting that these belonged to someone else.

I was silent and stayed submerged in the bathwater. He looked down at my body, as if to find the harshest punishment before using all his force, and stomping his foot on my stomach, uttering the words, 'This is useless. You can't even have kids.'

Within seconds, my wound opened, gushing with blood that turned the water red. I was in excruciating pain; my screams could be heard by all in the block. Seeing this, he panicked, and proceeded to call for an ambulance. I remained in hospital for another two weeks.

Whilst in hospital, I decided to leave him, but was going to plan it so he couldn't find and hurt me anymore. We never spoke of the incident again. I know he was ashamed of how he treated me. He was always sorry, there were many 'I will change, I won't do it again' moments, before the cycle began again. I was still planning my escape when the abuse started again.

My tolerance was wearing thin. One evening, I was taken to the edge. It was raining outside. I stood in the kitchen preparing dinner and for reasons I can't remember, an argument ensued. He started pushing me around the galley kitchen. He wanted a reaction from me, but I ignored him. The silence always got to him. He'd throw the odd jab at my face, then towards various parts of my body.

I'd had enough, in a loud assertive tone of voice, I said, 'You wanna kill me? Kill me! Finish it! 'Cause if you don't, I will.'

Those were my very words, as by then he had physically, psychologically and emotionally worn me down. I stopped caring about my existence in a nightmare of simply surviving. He pushed and pushed me into a corner, where I knocked against a knife block, which fell from the worktop. Seeing the sharp knives on the floor reminded me of our suspicions, which indicated bad news. Using all my will, I bent down and grabbed a knife, knelt on the floor and aimed it at my wrist, threatening to use it, if he didn't stop. I was ready to lose my life and didn't care anymore. He goaded me to do it, so without a second thought, pointing the sharp knife at my left wrist, I slid it across the bare skin, before dropping it to the floor.

I felt numb with shock. Was this how it ends? In total silence, we looked at each other for mere seconds, before I felt the warm blood trickling down. Pat's expression of urgency gave away that

I was bleeding. I expected to just fall and pass out. Instead, he stood me up, using a tea cloth pressed against my wrist.

I shouted, 'Don't touch me!'

As he stepped away, giving me a clear path, I saw this as my way out. Barefoot and still bleeding, I held tightly on to my wrist and ran out of the flat. Like Forest Gump, I just kept running. I didn't know if I was being chased, but I didn't care. I just kept running, down the corridor down the concrete stairs and finally into the street.

By now it was dark. It had been raining. I felt cold and dizzy. I was fortunate the cut wasn't too deep, but I needed help to safety. A young man from across the road saw the distress I was in and rushed over to offer help, initially suggesting we call an ambulance or the police, but I refused. I just wanted to go to Gert's house, where I knew I'd be safe. We found a telephone box and searched for her number in the phone book. The call was made and Gary came to fetch me. The young man stayed with me until he arrived. Although out of immediate danger, somehow I knew that it wasn't over. I knew Pat would find me and the abuse would start again.

# Chapter 10
# How We've Grown

My two-year toxic marriage greatly clouded my vision, festering in my own unhappy existence. Although unsure of my future, I knew changes were inevitable. Whilst married and living in London, I can't remember ever popping in for a coffee at Eric's, Marie's or Gert's, for that matter. It wasn't the done thing in our culture. Socialising was done mainly at an event. The lack of one-to-one contact prevented any of us from recognising our individual growth and struggles. We were judged mainly on how we were socially, and it's amazing how a deceptive smile can mask someone's grief.

For fear of him finding me I couldn't stay at Gert's place. Even though I knew they wouldn't mind, I didn't want to put on anyone unnecessarily. It was my problem and I needed to sort it. With fresh eyes, I was able to notice how some of us had grown, starting with Gert's and Gary's relationship, seeing how they lived with a growing family of two baby girls. They seemed preoccupied, but happy and settled, but not without their struggles. It would seem they accepted each other's flaws, which became the foundation for their long-lasting marriage.

After Marie and Jim were married, they, too, settled in London. Like Mum, Marie had old-fashioned values and wanted to be the perfect home-maker. They had three boys. I later learnt that she was desperate for a girl, but it wasn't to be. Her boys would go on to be hardworking and true gentlemen.

Eric, as we know, had a fair start in life, but still worked and studied just as hard to better himself and provide for his family. His loyal dedication and hard work saw him rise to a high level, and be rewarded with his own office. I once had the privilege to visit his work place; his private office overlooked an impressive view of the City of London. I felt so proud of him. Happily married to Rose with two children, I was made godmother to their firstborn, Dean. Like his dad, I knew he'd be successful; he has excelled above and beyond in the finance world. Eric's determination made sure his family values, alongside hard work and determination, would be instilled in both his children. His daughter Sabine is a beautiful, caring person, who holds many qualities and values that I admire. She reminds me a little of me in my younger years, full of life and laughter. Financially stable, Eric managed to retire at the age of 50. Together with Rose they continue to travel around the world, still enjoying life to the full.

Sensing I was being stalked by Pat outside my work caused me to move away and stay with the family in Northampton. At least I'd be safe, or so I thought. I couldn't drive back then, so I travelled up by coach, carrying very little baggage, I didn't know where they lived, but a taxi would get me to the address Gert had given me. As the coach pulled away from Victoria Station, I felt anxious, worried about their reaction to the real reason why I'd come. As far as they were concerned, all was well.

The coach journey was long and tiring. Wiping the mist away from the window, built up by condensation within, I got a glimpse of the outside. It got greener and greener as we travelled further out, and I could make out the odd farms, with sheep grazing on one and cows on others. The air appeared healthier. Far from what I'd become accustomed to, I kept thinking that he'd never find me here.

On arrival to Northampton coach station, everything seemed quieter. Northampton town was built around small villages, so it was new and still growing. I felt at ease after seeing a taxi rank across the road.

Feeling very nervous, I arrived at the huge three-storey, five-bedroom house. Mum opened the door.

With both my hands up in the air and a big smile, I shouted 'Surprise!', which was how I made my visit appear. The family was happy to see me. We laughed and talked for hours, but days after I told Mum that I needed a break after an argument that had resulted in him hitting me, but we never discussed the extent of the terrible things I suffered at his hands.

It was strange to be around my younger siblings again, noticing the changes. Our relationship was always superficial. Children generally spend time with their parents during childhood, but it was different for us; our separation didn't allow us to bond. The closeness in age made sibling rivalry particularly intense at times, but there was no real hatred or fights between us. We just never had deep conversations as a family or on a one-to-one level, but growing up, I imagine some of us formed opinions of one another. We were just children with the same parents, whose general love for us existed, but it was still never physically or verbally expressed. Speaking only for myself, seeing their struggle to keep food on the table was how I felt they cared and loved us.

The house was still hectic! The move to Northampton meant fewer house parties, but they would make up for it at every event, like birthdays, Christmas and so on. The younger ones continued entertaining themselves by demonstrating their ever-growing talents.

Dad was now retired. His daily routine after breakfast was to get ready for church. I'd watch him using a small plastic comb to comb his wispy hair to cover any thinning patch, followed by a habit of placing the comb back in his top pocket before putting on his beret. After mass, he'd walk across to the local shopping centre, where he'd spend a couple of hours in the betting shop for a flutter and a chat with the usual suspects, then head back, taking home Mum's favourite pecan pastry, just to keep her sweet. He was still enjoying his favourite tipple of whisky in the evenings.

I noticed Mum had started struggling with the stairs. She wasn't always in the best of health, but never really whinged about it. Her routine was repetitive. She'd come down in the morning and rarely went back up until it was time for bed. Her time was spent mainly in the kitchen and the dining room. She had taken up baking on a serious level, with regular orders for celebration cakes, and took joy in baking for the church. I'd sit and watch her decorate these cakes for hours and would at times give her a hand. Religion, to her, was key. She encouraged those at home to pray more, and of course some became altar boys at Great Billing Church. Once a month, a priest was invited over for dinner, either Father Diamond or Father Cannon.

Within a few weeks of being there, I liked the country air and the peace of living away from London. At least you'd be guaranteed a seat on the bus! I realised that living and working in London was very stressful and understood why Dad wanted to make the move. I, too, decided to make it my permanent home and find work.

My younger sister Mireille was working as an apprentice at John Richardson's hairdressing salon. We met in the town one afternoon, where I registered at Alfred Marks agency. A lovely Italian girl named Anna assisted us. She was friendly and even invited us round for coffee. A few days later, Mireille and I went to her place, where she introduced us to her husband Andrew and two brothers, John and Nick. They seemed kind, and we spent a few hours chatting and learning about each other's families. On our way out, one of them suggested we all go out one evening, which was fine with me, as it was a while since I'd been out socially. Sure enough, we met up and found ourselves at the Opus 2 nightclub. It felt great to be out. Still nervous at the thought that Pat might just turn up to make a scene, I had regular nightmares, and would often flinch at a sudden noise and movements that people made around me. That night, I kept looking over my shoulders, but as the evening wore on, I danced and laughed until my jaws ached.

Nick and Mireille seemed keen on one another; they continued to see each other for a while before she and a friend decided to take on some seasonal work at Butlins in Clacton-on-Sea. After her return, Nick became smitten with her, using every opportunity to see her. He was truly in love, which came as no surprise, as she was beautiful inside and out. They later married and had three girls. She is still a dedicated housewife and devotes her life to her family. I became godmother to their eldest daughter, Natasha, who's very switched on. I'm so proud of her achievements as a teacher. She is now happily married to Andrew, with three beautiful children.

Cecile had left home and rented a small flat close to where she worked as a nurse. She met and later married Lee and started a family straight away. They had three children. Unfortunately, their marriage ended in divorce. Cecile remains single to this day, dedicated to her faith, children and grandchildren. I'm happy to say that she never lost her spark, something that happens to many after a breakup, but she's still a happy-go-lucky character.

Jean Marc was always busy with his studies, but when it came to comedy, he'd let his guard down and entertain the family with hours of laughter. His key observations enabled him to imitate various popular characters on TV, and certain individuals within the family. His talents extended to playing the ravanne, a large tambourine-like instrument used in sega music from back home. His real passion was to make something of himself. I guess the poor foundation with regards to education made some of us determined to push ourselves more than others. He once contemplated becoming a priest, but gave up on the idea after meeting Kathlyn, whom he later married. They had two boys, who have now become very bright young men and complete their lives. I can honestly say that I admire his family, together with his great progressing career and recognition for his contribution, which finally saw him awarded with a Bachelor's degree in Leadership. Now Jean Marc is looking forward to his retirement after forty-one years in service.

François has always been an amusing character. He wanted to be seen as different, which would reflect on the way he dressed: odd but edgy. Like some of us, he experienced racial abuse at school, which caused him to develop a certain attitude and mannerism. If you didn't know him personally, his character would appear deranged. You would think he was suffering a seizure or some mental illness, screaming out and mumbling words that didn't make sense. It was a put-on to show that he wasn't one to mess with. This behaviour would be demonstrated when he felt danger looming, or so to not be picked on at school. At home, you'd see him move furniture and objects around the house, and place them oddly, where he thought it was more suited. The family just let him get on with it. He loved to dance and had an amazing voice. He and Shirley would sing beautiful duets.

After leaving school, François worked in a shoe factory for 11 years. Being good with his hands helped with the work that was required of him. However, his life was about to take a turn. At the age of twenty-one he felt a calling, after watching a film on the life of St Francis of Assisi. He left home at twenty-six taking a religious path in life on a three-year discernment. He was invited to become a Brother at The Oasis of Peace community in Italy, which is a semi-contemplative community that prays and promotes peace in the world. He later received his habit. When he entered the religious life, he was given a new name, and is now known as Frère Marie Irenee. It was expected of the Brothers to be moved to various Oasis of Peace communities around the world, so he found himself on a mission to Jamaica, where he was based for eight years. He then accepted another mission in Cameroon. This proved difficult at times, but he persevered with it. Four years ago, he was transferred to another community in Brazil. As well as it being The Oasis of Peace, it was also used as a centre for retreats, and many seminars are held where people are invited to participate in their activities. On his 25th anniversary of consecrated life, he received a blessing from Pope Francis. As a family, we're all proud of his dedication and achievement in life. I have always been amazed by his ability to speak five different languages. Everybody in the family now refers to him as Frère.

Popol was always reserved and you never knew what he was thinking. Still good-looking, he dreamt of being the next James Bond. He later married a lovely Jamaican girl named Cynthia, with two beautiful children, Jake and Jessica. The closest he got to being 007 was to work for the Civil Service, where he secretly operates...

Bernard was an easy-going character who never took himself seriously. Easy on the eye, everybody loved having him around, and there was never a dull moment when he showed up in the room. He'd greet you with his favourite saying, 'You make me laugh!' and was guaranteed to be the life and soul of the party, very much a spur-of-the-moment individual. In my view, he was the one that had changed the most. He wanted to be a body-builder and trained hard to enhance his physical appearance. Mireille's friend would come over to the house with her younger sister that Bernard took a liking to. They later married, and together had three children. Unfortunately, the eighteen-year marriage ended in divorce. He remarried and he lived for his family, friends and grandchildren. Sadly, his life was cut short after suffering a brain haemorrhage. We were all shocked and left devastated by the news. He would be the first amongst us to pass away, leaving a void in all our lives.

Shirley was still very shy and quiet, and would simply keep herself to herself. Nothing wrong with that, as I, too, loved my own space at times. She'd make an impression when it came to singing, as she also sang beautifully. She married young, but was left on her own to manage two young children. She later divorced; I believe she made the right choice, as they are better as friends. Her singing talent enabled her to follow a career by taking on seasonal contracts abroad, performing live in hotel lounges, bars and on cruises. When back home, she kept herself fit whilst working at the local gym. Shirley's life appears simple and she rarely complains about past choices she's made, which I respect and admire about her.

Peter adopted the nickname 'Johnny Reggae' for his obvious love of reggae music from his early teens. Mum started worrying about him, especially when he was out. He loved a laugh and at times would show off his talents of body popping, and confidently rap, making up his own sound. The dreadlocks completed his good looks. Unfortunately, he didn't like school much and would play truant, mixing with the wrong crowd. This would see him struggle in later life.

Things I remember clearly about Jacqueline: she was very close to Mum, with a certain confidence and somewhat cheeky with it. Being part of a musical family, it came to no surprise that she'd end up singing on a professional level. Growing up, you'd often hear her sing at the top of her voice alone in her room, and she was never without a bag of sweets in her hand. She'd sit on the end of my bed and watch me get ready, telling me she admired the way I applied my makeup. Jacqueline was still at school and was also having to deal with bullies, and at times Peter would intervene to protect her.

My life was also changing. I found work at a local printing firm as a telephonist/receptionist and looked for a place to rent. Knowing that Mum and Dad would wonder why I was settling, I decided to tell them the real reasons behind my move. After listening, Mum hoped that I'd rekindle with Pat. In their view, marriage was for life. It would be scandalous to divorce as a Catholic. Their pride couldn't see their child fail in a marriage.

Unfortunately, those old fashion values only work if you are prepared to become a punchbag. Failing to see how bad the situation was, Mum suggested speaking to Pat in the hope of bringing him to his senses. Still fearing him, I was in total disagreement. I came home from work one day, only to find him sitting in the dining room. Mum had written to him, suggesting that he came to make amends. You can imagine my anger. He simply wanted to talk and I had no choice but to listen to the same old apologies, this time trying to convince me to move back to London. Repeating the usual spiel, that his life was nothing without me, he'd change, and things would be better, blah, blah, blah! I told him that I was happy and settled, with no intention of leaving. He then suggested that he'd move to be closer, so we could start fresh.

I hear your thoughts as you read this. I know. Stupid, right? But a month or so later, Mum insisted I give him another chance. She convinced me that he'd be different, because they'd look out for me. Silly me went with it. Once he arrived in Northampton, he very quickly found a job at the local council. Believing he had changed and things would be better between us, I decided to give him a second chance. There were subtle changes; he seemed different and was more attentive. For a year or so, things did improve, and eventually we bought a place together. He even took me to Mauritius to make up for the honeymoon we never had.

Landing in Mauritius in the early hours after so many years, had it not been for the beautiful coastline in view whilst landing, you would think I'd landed somewhere else in Asia. The slow movements at passport controls allowed time to notice people more; there appeared to be an obvious higher population of Hindus and Muslims. Travelling from the airport, you couldn't help notice the island's beauty, with rolling hills, and dense rainforest that extends for miles across, which I admit when growing up I took for granted. Seeing the sugar cane fields made me smile; I was excited, knowing I'd come home. When growing up I hadn't seen much on the outside, but I'm sure I would have noticed the brilliantly coloured Hindu statues with accents of gold of various gods and temples dotted around the villages and towns that seemed to overpower other significant landmarks on the island.

Whilst there, it was inevitable that I'd attempt to visit my past. Our family home had been renovated; I had to look twice as it had changed so much. Everything seemed smaller, but the château was still just as impressive.

Stella and Monique took me to visit the convent. I didn't know if I was ready to go there again, but it was an opportunity I couldn't resist. The structure seemed small and insignificant. I learnt it was no longer an orphanage., I managed to see a few nuns, but none from when we were there. Standing in the grounds brought back many bad memories. I couldn't help looking across towards the metal gate with the steps that led to the basse-cour. I didn't want to walk down there or see other areas we'd spent time in. Honestly, I just wanted to leave.

Walking through the yard as we were leaving, I felt sad looking down at where I was severely punished. Thinking of Ursulle breaking her arm at the bottom of the steps reminded me of my promise to her. I had to find her, together with the family that tried to adopt me. I asked the nun if they could assist and they said they'd make enquiries and let me know.

Monique managed to trace Ursulle, and I was so excited at the thought of seeing her again. Pat and I travelled by taxi to an address that was odd, with no number. We arrived in a shanty village of the poorest part of the island, far from the picture you have of polished beach-front hotel complexes. With rubbish strewn around, the area looked dirty and it felt unsafe. Seeing underfed stray dogs roaming freely in the area, I didn't recognise the island I'd left behind.

Had I been a tourist, the sight would have certainly turned me off. As the driver slowly drove through the red earth dirt track, children ran up to the car and within seconds we were surrounded. Others stood on their makeshift porches holding babies on their hips, looking at us with suspicion. The driver, standing by the taxi, was no help. He told us that they rarely drove to the area and, further, that many Chagossians lived in the area. I didn't fully understand who he meant exactly, and ignored the comments and information that would one day become significant.

Looking around, the poverty was evident. Children appeared undernourished. Our knowledge of the native tongue helped when we had to ask for directions to Ursulle's place, thinking her surname was still the same. An old lady pointed across to where she thought was the place, which looked similar to others around, built from scrap wood and corrugated sheeting.

Now at her door, unsure of what to expect, I knocked. She peered through the thin plyboard door, which was slightly ajar, frowning, looking confused and not knowing who we were. I didn't recognise her either and for a split second I wondered if we had the right person. I tried to get a closer look at her face and told her who I was. The door opened wider and I gave her a friendly smile. She studied my face for a few seconds. Had it not been for her unmissable smile, which gave her away, I would have never recognised her. I could hear a baby crying in the background and I told her I'd kept my promise to find her.

This made her weak at the knees; she was clearly in shock. I had bought a doll to say sorry for breaking her arm. There followed a mixture of laughter and tears, neither of us knowing how to be with the other. She lifted her son from a bucket that she used as a cot; he wouldn't stop crying, clearly hungry. Looking around, I couldn't see any toys, so I gave him the doll, which stopped him crying for a minute or so.

Their living conditions were poor. She apologised for not being able to offer us anything to drink, which we didn't care about. I just wanted to hear her voice and have her tell me all that happened after I left the convent. Similarly, I told her of our lives back in the UK. Ursulle was now married and her husband was working in the field. She wanted us to meet him, so Pat suggested that they dine with us later on that evening. Her husband was happy to meet us. We treated them to a slap-up meal at the nicest restaurant on the coast.

The next day, I took clothes and food for her and her son. She heard that we didn't have children of our own. As we were leaving, tears streaming down her face, holding her baby with stretched arms towards me, begging in desperation:

'Please, please, take him. We can't afford to care for him. We're poor, he'll die here.'

Pat and I looked at one another in disbelief, then I told her that it wasn't realistic. Although desperate to have a child of our own, I could never separate this baby from his family. Instead, we gave them enough money to help with the month's shopping. It was sad to see them living like that. We said our goodbyes and promised to stay in touch. We kept in touch for a while, until the letters were returned to sender. I later found out that her village had been destroyed by flash floods caused after a terrible cyclone and the inhabitants had been relocated. I never heard from her again. Did she lose my address? I know that can happen.

Unfortunately, I didn't manage to make contact with the couple who wanted to adopt me. I desperately wanted to apologise for losing their address. I did always think about them, but fate had a way of circling back.

**My graduation**

**Myself and baby
Zoyla donned in
Navajo style for a
photo shoot**

**Family photo at Eric and Roselys' wedding**

**Jacqui Berne at the height of her singing career**

**My social life with close friends**

**Our complete family; celebrating Dad's 70th birthday. Taken in age order, left to right: Dad, Mum, Eric, Marie, Gertrude, Danielle, Cecile, Jean-Marc, Mireille, Francois, Popol, Bernard, Shirley, Peter, and Jacqueline**

**Eternity ring from Mark**

**A favourite from my modelling portfolio**

**Arlena, Cameron and
Jasper the dog**

**Brothers and sisters**

**The next generation (grandchildren)**

**Mum and Dad as
we remember them**

**Michelle, the kind lady
who wanted to adopt me**

**Hair modelling**

# Chapter 11
# Social Butterfly

Back in the UK, life continued, with us doing our best to keep a happy marriage. Various tests were carried out as to why I couldn't bear children. I was told I was born with only one fallopian tube, which would make it more difficult, but not impossible. Pat wasn't keen to take a test and left it down to me, stupidly resigning myself to thinking that I'd never have children.

Over the next few years as a couple, we managed to create some lovely memories. The family was welcoming and enjoyed having him around. Taking up new hobbies of mixing cocktails and experimenting with Chinese cooking gave me the confidence to host many dinner parties. I even started collecting old vinyl records and matchboxes from all over the world.

Evolving with a new look, hair slightly tinted, styled in the ever-popular Farrah Fawcett look, boosted my confidence, resulting in more male attention, especially from men at work, which I mainly ignored, but Pat would notice this. When he picked me up from work, I found myself having to justify certain things, like the way I dressed, my makeup, etc. The same old alarm bells were ringing. I soon realised that we were arguing about the silliest things around the house, especially when items were not kept where they should be. His OCD had become more obsessive and was the main cause of the arguments. I would be asked to explain my movements, who I was with and where I went. I found myself lying to him, just to keep the peace. It was apparent that his jealousy hadn't completely left him.

One afternoon, whilst walking in town, I was stopped by a hairdresser from a well-known salon in the area. She asked if I would be interested in featuring in a hair magazine. I agreed to do so: anything for a free haircut, not to mention I needed a bit of pick-me-up, as my marriage was on the rocks again. Although I felt great after having been given a new look, these changes caused his jealousy to resurface and the arguments continued.

One day, things ended with him striking me again. This time the beating was horrific, with punches and kicks to the stomach and face whilst I crouched on the floor between the bed and the wardrobe. Seeing my life flash before me, I was once again in danger. All I could think of, was, *how do I get away?* I was left in pain, silently sobbing and rocking myself to sleep. The next morning, my whole body ached. I wasn't feeling well enough to go to work, but didn't want to stay home either. With a bruised, puffed-up face and a big black eye, I struggled into work, hoping no one would notice: difficult to avoid, given I was the first point of contact as the company's receptionist.

Wearing ridiculous sunglasses obviously brought attention to me. I had barely removed my coat before I was called into the office to discuss what they feared. I tried to make an excuse for the way I looked, but they weren't silly and wanted to help. I was instructed to wait in another room, for I couldn't sit at reception in that condition.

That very morning, two police officers came to see me at work, concerned. They wanted to get to the truth and felt it was their duty to intervene. After questioning me, they explained their actions, and how they would help put a stop to the abuse. It was to be done in a way that didn't reflect on me involving them. I was asked to go back home and act as normal, and to expect a visit from them that evening. They planned to come round and have an informal chat, after which they'd wait in the car park until they felt I wasn't in any immediate danger. I agreed, after being reassured.

The doorbell rang.

Pat looked at me. 'Are you expecting anyone?'

I simply replied, 'No.'

He went to open the door, whilst I remained sat silently in the lounge. The same officers walked in and I didn't move.

Looking across at me, the male officer commented, 'That's a real shiner you have there, young lady.'

Turning to Pat, the officers' posture and mannerisms changed, using a certain tone of voice.

'Hope you didn't have anything to do with that, 'cause if you did, your feet won't touch the ground, matey,'

At that, Pat denied having anything to do with it.

The officer added, 'Look, we've had a complaint from a neighbour. It seems there were disturbing noises coming from this house last night, so we're here to look into it.'

At this, Pat asked, 'Who?'

The officer replied, 'I'm not at liberty to say, but I warn you, if I have to come back here, it won't be to have a chat.'

At this point, not knowing what Pat's reaction would be, I was bracing myself for the worst. Before leaving, the female officer looked over at me, with a reassuring grin. After shutting the door behind them, Pat silently made his way upstairs. Through the half-opened curtain, I could see the reflection of spotlights coming from the car park. I knew they hadn't left.

It was to be the last time he ever laid hands on me. The damage had been done and I was left feeling numb. Any trust and respect I held for him died that very day, which made it easy to detach myself emotionally. The embarrassment didn't make me feel good about working for the same firm. Shortly after, I found another job working as a sales assistant for Radio Rentals at Weston Favell Shopping Centre.

Any man who would come after would find it hard to gain my trust, and would rarely be given a second chance. My slow lessons in life were taking form, leading me towards how I'd choose to live in the future. I didn't see the point in being married, so I asked for a divorce. I didn't care what anyone thought. He suggested seeing a marriage counsellor. At first, I didn't want anything to change my mind, but went along anyway. There, we discussed my past and my lack of feelings for him. They thought that my being abandoned as a child was the core issue, and was recognised that I would hurt those by leaving before they left me. I didn't see it that way because I was ready to give 100% loyalty to anyone sharing my life.

I wasn't able to leave before the house was sold, but Pat respected my space. We lived under the same roof and slept in separate rooms. When it was time I left, taking just my personal belongings. I didn't want anything to remind me of my life with him. Starting from fresh, I rented a small flat close to my job. I even joined the local gym. I quickly settled into my new role, making new friends. I was finally free and making up for the lost years. Jacqueline's school was nearby, and she'd spend every lunch break visiting me at work. It was the beginning of my close bond with her.

With very little to do after work, the gym became my favourite pastime. There, I caught the attention of a young lifeguard named Chris. Apparently, he'd been eyeing me up since clocking me wearing a bright yellow polka-dot swimsuit. Noticing only his good looks and great physique was as far as it went. His attraction to me had gone totally unnoticed, and was only realised when I tried to fix him up with a work colleague.

He pulled me to one side and said, 'It's you I'm interested in.'

I gave him the brush, saying, 'You're too young!' but he had no intention of giving up, and patiently waited for months, before I eventually agreed to go out for a drink.

I realised he was quite mature and good company. I liked the idea of having him around, but not before making it clear that we'd be history if he attempted to hurt me in any way.

I went on holiday with Jacqueline for two weeks, but on my return I noticed a change in his behaviour, especially around young girls. He'd openly chat them up in front of me. It didn't take much to convince me that I was wasting my time, so I ended it with him. Simple. No regrets, but we remained friends.

From then on, without looking for a relationship, younger men would just pop up in my life. A few weeks later, a young police officer noticed me whilst working at a different branch in the town. He was smitten from the word go. He'd try to get my attention by walking past the window every day. He even attempted to sign a contract to rent the latest TV model. He was tall, fair and handsome, with a Robert Redford look about him. After a while, I gave in and agreed to go out with him.

It was nice. We spent nearly two years together before he popped the question. The feeling that someone loves you enough to want to marry you is comforting. It made me feel wanted and desired, but on our way to choose the ring, my gut instincts were telling me that it wasn't right. I thought my feelings for him were love, but I questioned why I was getting the jitters. Could it be because he had a jealous side to him? Who knows, but I made an excuse and sat in the public toilets for perhaps a little too long. When I resurfaced, no explanation was needed; he just knew I wasn't ready. This doubt made both of us question the strength and seriousness of our relationship, which eventually ended.

I should have been upset, because I genuinely felt something for him. I had an epiphany moment, when I realised I was a happier person outside a relationship. Enjoying my own space and freedom, life was stress-free and uncomplicated, but I needed to make it count for something. I travelled and spent quality time with friends, who were becoming an important factor in my life. However, whether male or female, I was always careful who I mixed with. I had to trust them fully before letting them in.

A mutual friend introduced me to Mark, who was young, energetic and proved to be a real gentleman. Very popular and socially well connected, when I'd see him out, he'd treat me more like his little sister and looked out for me. I got to know his family, who were welcoming and kind. After Mark emigrated to America, his mum Ann would become a good friend of mine. Most of the friends I made were female but Paul was another I considered a good mate; he was kind and didn't take me for granted. I can honestly say I spent many hours having interesting and meaningful conversations with him.

Certain individuals would describe me as a social butterfly, because I shone in a crowded room. I adopted the motto 'The more the merrier'. I guess it's true; I do like being in the spotlight, but I also had my down days that would see me become a real introvert at times. Time became another valuable factor, possibly because I lost so much of it, so I'd spend it wisely and meaningfully. Even though I like to plan, I would change my mind quite often, so if something sounded more inviting or fun, of course, I would opt for the more exciting option. However, this mind-changing has cost me dearly in the past. Like butterflies, I don't stick around for long.

However, generally, life was never dull. My weekends would run from Wednesday through to Sunday.

Jo was a glamorous, tall blonde, who stood out in the crowd. We instantly gelled after meeting for the first time at Ritzy nightclub. She had a witty sense of humour and was fun to be around. We'd go on to spend some memorable girlie holidays together. She was hard working and owned a small clothing business. At times, I would be called to model these at events, to be sold on the day at various venues.

It was now the mid-80s. Jaqueline had just turned sixteen. Whilst performing at a school concert, she was noticed by a young entrepreneur named Simon Shine. He was captivated by her voice and instantly recognised her talents as a potential recording artist. He arranged to meet Mum and Dad to discuss her singing career, with a possible record deal. It would mean she'd have to stay in London to record songs. Because of her young age, Dad was totally against the idea, but they were left to think about it. I too, believed in her potential and didn't want her to miss out on what seemed to be a genuine opportunity. Knowing already what that was like, I felt I should intervene to avoid a what-if and if-only regrets in her life.

I tried to get Mum and Dad to see sense and even suggested that I'd chaperone her in London. They eventually agreed to let her go. Jacqueline moved to Maida Vale and stayed in Simon's flat. Under the guidance of professionals, she learned all there was to become a professional singer. In creating her new image, they kept her busy with dancing lessons and voice training sessions. She adopted a stage name: Jacqui Berne. Once they felt she was ready, she began recording songs at Red Bus studios, followed by many photoshoots and video recordings to promote her. Despite her talents, getting a record deal was proving harder, so Simon launched his own label and called it Hi Hat Records. Within the first year, she was being recognised as a young artist. Her music proved more successful in Europe and the USA. She had a hit with the cover song 'It's Been So Long', together with various others that had been written solely for her. She was now at her peak and loving the experience.

My active social life was teaching me a lot about people in general, becoming more streetwise and recognising the dangers associated with nightlife. I wasn't one for drinking or taking drugs, but it was clearly out there. Witnessing those being destroyed whilst making it their scene taught me to avoid it at all costs. I didn't care much for anyone involved in crime, either.

Realising there was more to life, I focused on using every opportunity to educate myself further, broadening my horizons with various courses being offered whilst working at Radio Rentals. Having a good manager helped. She once encouraged me to enrol on a BTEC in Marketing and Management. Not only did it teach me about leadership, but it also opened my eyes to other areas of my own background. Part of the course would require me to participate in an audience assessment, with a presentation of choice. Although I was comfortable in a crowded room and liked being in the spotlight, this was different. Public speech was something I lacked confidence in.

Mum and Dad could see my struggles in choosing a topic and naturally wanted to help. I couldn't see how, but Dad came up with the idea of a presentation on the economy of Mauritius, which naturally meant I needed to know all there was about the island. The more I researched, the more interesting the subject became. Mum and Dad would tell me as much as they could, which opened up other areas on a more personal level. As a family we rarely spoke about the past, but Dad knew my inquisitive side would naturally want to know more, so whilst taking note, we discussed how they met, the extended family, their friends and work colleagues back home, and ultimately why they left. Suddenly, it was all starting to make sense, which filled the gaps in my childhood memory and, of course, how we ended up in the UK.

More importantly, I learnt about the shift in government that started it all, which led me to research more on the subject. For the first time, I took an interest in what the Indian Ocean was about, and in particular the Chagos Archipelago that formed over sixty unique coral islands, one of the largest being Diego Garcia, and the shocking reality of what happened to the Chagossians and what led them to Mauritius. I felt guilty for ignoring the taxi driver's comment about this nation when I'd visited Ursulle. I'm am a great believer in fate and would soon find myself connected to them somehow. It did make me wonder why Ursulle ended up living in the area. She had told me her family was lost in a house fire, so maybe her husband was originally from the Chagos Islands.

It took three months to prepare before delivering my presentation, after which someone suggested I should write a book about it. The idea stayed on the back burner for many years, until now. My ambition was recognised when I was given the opportunity to be the sales manager, with a company car. Unable to drive, I took a crash course and passed within a month. I couldn't afford anything but a second-hand car, and I found myself manoeuvring a heap of junk back and forth to work. Within weeks, I suffered a terrible accident on the A45 dual carriageway.

It was completely my fault – my lack of knowledge and ignorance – for driving at speed with no threads on the tyres. The wet, slippery conditions didn't help. Whilst attempting to change lanes, I found the car spinning as though it was in a washing machine, before colliding with a concrete lamp post, which landed across the carriageway, causing the busy traffic to come to a halt. The incident was so serious it made the evening news. I should have died there and then, but regained consciousness in hospital with only minor injuries. Someone was definitely looking down on me that day.

I was living for moments that were particularly memorable. I once organised a family showcase in a village hall filled with extended family and friends, who brought along food and drinks. I had created a stage to put on a fashion show, which my friend Jo helped with, hosted by Jean Marc, who was also in charge of comedy sketches, with singing duets and dancing competitions. Jacqueline was now a professional and featured as the main star of the evening. Four of the brothers gave a convincing performance as The Shadows. Finally, my imitation of Tina Turner singing 'Simply the Best' was the biggest surprise, as it was so unexpected. The whole event would be remembered and talked about for years to come. Mum and Dad lived for moments like these. That evening, as well as their laughter, you could also see the pride and happiness on their faces as they watched their children in action. It became the main reason why we regularly organised theme nights on a similar scale.

The extra time spent with Jacqueline throughout her singing career made our bond even stronger. It didn't matter that there was a twelve-year age gap between us. We enjoyed the same things, and would often go out in the town and spend girlie holidays together. She had many school friends. Her fame made her popular around the town. In turn, I became familiar with her friends, who were obviously much younger, but kept me young and in with the times.

One summer, Jacqueline and I spent a memorable holiday in Ibiza, dancing on the podium and making the most of it. The hotel suffered a blackout following a storm during the night. The staff had lit candles in the corridors and stairwell to assist those wandering around still. Going down for breakfast the next morning and oblivious to this, I noticed an old lady at the bottom of the staircase. It appeared she had fallen. I shouted down to see if she was okay, reassuring her that I was coming to help, but before I reached the bottom, I too slipped and landed right next to her. Our fall was caused after we both slipped on old candle wax on the steps. We waited for the ambulance, both in excruciating pain, then were taken to the local hospital. I had a broken fibula, so a cast was fitted from the knee down to my toes. With four days left this ruined our holiday, but we would laugh about it later.

After flying back home, I carried on working, but days later I collapsed at work and was rushed to hospital. It seemed that I had suffered a DVT. On removing the cast, my foot was very swollen and badly bruised. I was given the news that my foot had been wrongly set and needed to be broken again and reset. *Who does that?* was my instant thought. No need to describe the pain; I'll leave that to your imagination. I was to spend a few more days in hospital.

My recovery was slow, and couldn't wait to go out for a good knees-up. When ready to party again, Jacqueline and I went around town in fancy dress. The theme was beachwear, with flowers in our hair, the works. Confidently strolling into bars down Bridge Street. Had I not heard a particular man's colourful comments, which cannot be repeated here, I wouldn't have clocked him standing at the entrance. His remarks made him unappealing and pathetic.

Not long after, finding myself at Knights Club, there he was again. This time he was trying to catch my attention. I won't lie, he had a certain charm, although he was much younger than me. I entertained him chatting me up before agreeing to a dance. I had forgotten his name, and would talk about him to friends, describing him as looking like the lead singer from INXS. It was the name I adopted for him from then on. I'd casually see him around the town, and would say 'Oh look! There's INXS.'

Within a short time, I found myself in a relationship with him, even though the signs of him being a womaniser were there and heartbreak was going to be inevitable. To this day, I ask myself why. This is something that many of us question in our lives, and you cannot control the fate that lies in store for you.

Around the same time, Jacqueline met a young attractive man named Shaun, whose work as a sports photographer took him away for weeks on end. They became besotted with one another. As far as she was concerned, they were in love. During his trips away, Jacqueline would concentrate on her singing, which kept her busy. She spent two weeks in New York at Rick Wakeman's house, who was producing one of her songs, 'Celebrate'. It proved popular on high-energy charts. On their return to London, Simon decided to sign Cindy Birdsong (from The Supremes) on his record label. Jacqueline felt he was investing more into that particular artist and not promoting her enough.

Simon's interest in Jacqueline shifted from the role of manager to a more personal level. He once expressed his wish to marry her. She made it obvious that the feeling was not mutual and she wanted to keep it professional, after which she felt some resentment when her contract wasn't renewed. Moving back to Northampton, Jacqueline continued singing at clubs like Ronnie

Scott's in London and various others, until she called it a day, settling for a meaningful relationship with Shaun.

# Chapter 12
# One Small Miracle

I too had started seeing the INXS guy; it was to be a casual thing. He was still a young man about town, leading a very active social life, but although we liked each other, neither of us was looking to settle down. He enjoyed time with his mates; I suspected he enjoyed the ladies, too. I wasn't one to waste time in relationships, so at the slightest disagreement it was easy for me to walk away. After a very short time together, I decided to call it a day, as the relationship seemed pointless. Maybe the counsellors were right about me leaving people before they hurt me. However, months later, feeling a change in my body and concerned after a couple of missed periods, friends advised me to take a pregnancy test, which I dismissed at first. As far as I was concerned, I couldn't fall pregnant - something I had told him, so no protection was used.

Thinking hard about the possibility led me to take a test whilst on my lunch break. I asked Jacqueline to be there for the results, and to our surprise the strip changed to pink, indicating it was positive. I can't explain the mixture of emotions running through me all at once, before hitting me like a ton of bricks.

Looking up at Jacqueline, I said, 'I'm pregnant.'

Jacqueline jumped up and down with excitement, whilst my thoughts turned to Mum and Dad. *How am I going to tell them? I mean, they didn't even know I was seeing anyone. What would they think? Worst of all, I had left him! How am I going to tell him?* Then reality set in. *My life will no longer be the same. My ambition at work: what about work, the BTEC course I was hoping to complete and graduate?* All those thoughts were running through my mind.

It took me days to process the whole situation. I had to tell Mum. In doing so, her reaction wasn't what I expected.

She lifted her arms up in the air, and shouted, 'It's a miracle!'

I said, 'No, there was a man involved. It wasn't an immaculate conception!'

She didn't seem to care how it happened, but was more relieved that her daughter was able to have children. I eventually told her about the father.

Obviously, he had to know, but I didn't want him to be with me just because I was expecting his child. The bottom line was, there was no love between us. He was happy to hear the news and naturally wanted to play a part in the child's life. As my tummy grew, his fatherly duty was also growing, but I was happy to bring up the baby alone.

I continued working and I'm glad to say completed the BTEC course and graduated with a certificate of excellence whilst six months pregnant, with every intention of continuing my role after maternity leave. Unfortunately, at 27 weeks, I went into early labour. Apparently, the umbilical cord was wrapped around the baby's neck, causing distress. An emergency C-section was carried out under general anaesthetic, after which they made me conscious long enough to see her dad holding her, looking across at me.

He said, 'It's a girl,' before I was out again.

Opening my eyes in the early hours, instead of the usual thoughts like *what shall I wear for work today?*, the effects of the anaesthetic reminded me why I was there. Waking up in a panic, eyes twitching right to left in search of a baby's crib, which should have been next to me, I shouted for the nurse.

'Where's my baby?'

She rushed over, and tried to console me by explaining how poorly the baby was. In fact, her condition was critical and she was fighting for her life in intensive care. I cried and cried, behaving as though I'd already lost her. Insisting that I needed to see her, hours later, they wheeled me into Gosset Ward, a neonatal intensive care unit.

Unable to hold or touch her, I simply had to watch her through a clear plastic incubator, seeing her rapid shallow breathing clearly indicating her struggles. The woollen bonnet was far too big for her tiny head. Her frail wrinkly body showed the lack of fat and how premature she was. Although the tubes and wires attached to her were there for a good reason, I couldn't help but see it as barbaric. The nurse explained that her lungs had not properly developed, which was causing the erratic breathing aided by a ventilator. Feeling a deep guilt, I saw it as punishment. For what? I couldn't tell you.

I was wheeled back to the ward after experiencing pain in my leg and finding it hard to breathe. I put it down to stress or possibly a panic attack, but after suffering more pains across my chest, I was being cared for on an emergency level. It became apparent that I had suffered a blood clot on the lungs, possibly caused by the surgery. We were both hanging on for dear life. I was attached to various machines and wires, which made it impossible for me to see her for a while, and when I did, I was told that she had good and bad days. The main problem was feeding. I felt a failure for not being able to express any milk; that had dried up partly through stress. As it turned out, the medication I was being treated with meant it wouldn't have been suitable. She was holding on by a thread.

Family members would come along and spend time with me in the hospital chapel, praying for my baby's recovery. Totally dependent on oxygen and still needing a lot of care, she was fragile and weak, with hit and miss moments, but it seems she was a fighter. Slowly achieving milestones over the weeks. She grew strong enough to cope without a ventilator, giving enough time to hold her. The feeling was truly amazing. That's when I gave her the name Zoyla, which had stayed with me all those years.

Her dad still wanted to be part of our lives, although I felt that bringing up a child together wouldn't improve our relationship. I didn't feel he was prepared to take on the responsibility to be more committed. However, I knew my own feelings had changed after giving birth, so perhaps he also felt different. I agreed for Zoyla's sake to give him the benefit of doubt. It wasn't about me anymore; I was a Mum who needed to care for her fragile baby girl.

Finally, we were able to take her home. We'd watch her for hours as she slept. Her dad couldn't keep his eyes off her; he was truly proud to be a dad. He'd spend time holding her for as long as he could, taking turns to feed her.

A week or so later, I was feeding her alone when I noticed her lips were slightly blue in colour. In my panic, I wrapped her up, holding her tightly in my arms and ran half a mile to our doctor's surgery. I don't know why I didn't call for an ambulance, but my instincts told me to run for help. Luckily, she was seen straight away, and ended up in hospital, where she remained for a week before coming home.

We moved into a three-bedroom house, and for a couple of months tried to be a family. He decorated the baby's room beautifully, but that's as far as it went. His lack of support and attention was obvious, which caused many arguments between us. He'd make promises to change, but I'd had enough of the empty promises, making it easier for me to call it a day. This decision may have appeared harsh to some, and perhaps I wasn't doing my daughter any favours, but it was unfair for us both to continue in a dead-end relationship just for her sake. I was already caring for her as though I was a single mum, so the decision to leave him was to focus on being a good, happy mum instead of a miserable one.

After every failed relationship, I would physically and emotionally detach myself, building a protective wall around me, each time a little bit higher than the last, at times, reinforced with defences that made me appear harsh. Disappointed with my poor judgements in life, I found it hard to find balance in a loving relationship. The answers weren't clear, but I knew I was a better person alone, and would do everything possible to protect myself and my child.

By the time my maternity leave was up, Zoyla still needed a lot of care and my own health had been compromised, so I didn't continue my job at Radio Rentals. I concentrated on her care, making sure she grew strong and healthy, while at the same time providing her with as much love as possible, because her dad wasn't around. In fact, he had decided to work abroad.

Zoyla would often be seen in A&E with breathing difficulties. In the first seven years of her life, she was asthmatic and used an inhaler. In her early childhood, she had little contact with her dad, but would regularly see his family. She became particularly fond of her nan.

It was a normal weekday, when I was out shopping at Weston Favell centre and rushing around with Zoyla in the pushchair, a lady stopped me in my tracks, and said, 'Hi! You're perfect for our magazine. Would you mind coming with me?'

I was all baffled and didn't really know what she was asking. I said, 'Look, my little one will need feeding soon, so I really don't have much time,' but she insisted it wouldn't take long and I was to follow her whilst she explained what they were trying to achieve.

At the time, *The Clothes Show* was travelling to various towns and cities in the UK, to promote a fashion tourist calendar, giving shoppers an opportunity to be immersed in the glamorous world of fashion. They were using the first letter of each town to create a theme and Northampton was to focus on the Navajo. I guess the modelling scout who spotted me thought I had the look.

They worked quickly on my hair and makeup, before dressing me up. By then Zoyla was crying, so they got me to hold her all wrapped up in a Navajo blanket, which completed the look and we both featured in their December issue.

Like me, Zoyla developed a curious and inquisitive mind; she would want me to constantly read bedtime stories. Her favourite was *Chugga Chugga Choo Choo*. I'd read this book until it sent me to sleep, but she'd still be awake wanting more. She never wanted to miss out on anything and lived for parties and family gatherings. At the age of two, she wanted to leave home after being upset, because it was her bedtime. Although funny at the time, it hurt that she would want to leave me.

I needed to keep our heads above water and was keen to make a living, so I took in foreign students to bring in extra income. At the same time, I was given an opportunity to teach at a local language school. I qualified as a TEFL teacher and taught intermediate-level English as a second language. I also started a small business, initially selling accessories, which proved more successful after venturing into clothing, enabling me to buy a decent car and apply for a mortgage on a house. I was self-sufficient; there was little anyone could offer me. I wasn't rich, but I coped financially.

A few years on, a friend suggested I worked too hard and needed some fun in my life. She convinced me to go on a blind date with her neighbour. I wasn't keen on the idea, but eventually gave in to it. On meeting him for the first time, I can't say there was an initial attraction, but within weeks he tried hard to win me over, using every romantic gesture to do so. Realising I lived mainly for my daughter, he'd often suggest that we go out as a family, demonstrating his caring side, and clearly wanting to show how good a dad he'd be.

Bringing down part of my protective wall would leave me vulnerable, but it allowed me to appreciate his romantic gestures, which were clearly lacking in my life. He seemed perfect, or at least I desperately wanted him to be so. Of course, when he proposed, although a bit too soon, it felt natural to go with it. Six months later, I found myself walking up the aisle, and after renting out my place I was moving in with him. Three months later, I was expecting, which we were both happy about, but not long after, it started to go downhill. Things weren't quite right. I stumbled across a pack of lies surrounding his life and finances. When confronted with it all, initially he tried to deny it, but eventually came clean. This lack of trust didn't allow me to feel the same again.

Nine years of my life were stolen in my first marriage. I wasn't about to waste any more of my precious time trying to make this one right. Once again, the decision was easy to leave. I knew I was a good mum and was ready to go it alone. Throughout my life, it was apparent the only thing men brought to the table was pain and deceit. I walked out of a second marriage, with very little. I even left my clothes behind.

Now I had to rebuild my life, but this time with another child on the way. When it was time to give birth, a C-section was advised, because of possible complications. Along with that, the doctor thought that having more children would be risky, so I agreed to have my one fallopian tied. I gave birth to Arlena and luckily, she was born healthy. She shares the name of a beautiful Latino model. When I first laid eyes on her, all I could see was a mass of jet-black hair. She looked like Mowgli from *The Jungle Book*, so cute. Her dad was a doting father and would play a big part in her life. He really loved and cared for her. I couldn't fault him as a dad.

Unfortunately, for me, whilst still in hospital, I suffered yet another pulmonary embolism. Because of this recurrence, I was to remain on lifelong treatment. Soon after leaving the hospital, I suffered further complications with internal bleeding, causing a pelvic haematoma and found myself back in hospital. The doctors couldn't operate so soon after the C-section, so another surgery was scheduled for later that year.

On reflection, the bad decisions I made in life only caused pain and suffering, when all I wanted was to love and be loved. I was a good person and ready to be a loyal wife, and certainly never doubted my abilities to be a good mum. I took accountability for my wrong judgements, making sure my girls weren't going to pay the price. I protected them in a bubble. My ill health caused me to stop work, which had a negative impact. I did the best I could for my girls, devoting my entire existence to creating a safe and loving environment for them both. I made sure they didn't go without, feeding them before myself, in the same way Mum and Dad had done to express their love and care for us.

November 1993, and it was time to have surgery to remove the pelvic haematoma. Although risky, it was my only option. All the care would be taken for it to run smoothly. Afterwards, I was left to recover in a private room. As I came to, the lights were dim and I was being monitored by a machine that was constantly beeping, and I was attached to various drips and pumps, which made me realise I was having a blood transfusion. Lifting my head slightly, I could see Dad all alone sat in a chair, praying on a bright yellow rosary.

He didn't say much, just watched me for a while, before leaning over, handing me his beads, saying, 'I'll see you again tomorrow.'

I kept falling in and out of consciousness. Feeling a sudden chill, I peered over to see a lady standing at the end of the bed, her head slightly bent over one shoulder. She was trying to say something, but I couldn't make it out. She looked unwell and I thought she might have been another patient. I tried to lift my head to get a closer look, but became distracted when my movement caused the rosary to fall from the bed. Seconds later, I looked up and realised she was no longer there.

I felt cold, with excruciating pain in my stomach, which was so bloated, as though I was about to give birth again. I pressed for more morphine, but the pain continued. I pressed the bell for assistance and moments later a nurse appeared. She rushed towards the windows, saying, 'Who left these open? It's so cold in here!'

I knew it wasn't me, but didn't think much more about it. With the main lights on, she noticed I didn't look right, and quickly sounded the alarm for extra assistance. Minutes later, my vital obs and blood were being taken with nurses, doctors and consultants gathered around the bed. I was being prepared to go back into theatre.

The pain was unbearable as they wheeled me to theatre, gazing at the white ceiling above, before seeing my consultant Mr Bibi, standing alongside a priest, who was there to anoint, and give me the last rites.

Mr. Bibi held my hands tightly and said, 'I will do all I can. Be brave and strong.'

At that, I felt a sudden calm; the pain had gone. I could still see everyone in the room all geared up in their scrubs, having conversations between themselves. Mr Bibi was bent looking over me, before opening me up. I couldn't understand or tell you why I could see all this without feeling any pain. I simply watched them working on me.

The next thing I remember was waking up in the same private room, this time with family members next to me. Arlena's dad was there, too, and reassured me that the girls were okay.

Mum was crying as she approached to kiss me on the cheeks, and said, 'You should know that Liseby died last night.'

I replied, 'I think, I saw her.'

She said, 'No, you couldn't have; she died in hospital in London.'

I said, 'I think she came to see me.'

Mum looked at me in a strange way, I believed she knew I wasn't lying. Liseby was the aunt I admired so much, when she came to the convent to tell us the good news that we would all soon be reunited with Mum and Dad.

A young hospital worker popped his head round and said, 'I was working on your blood results last night, and needed to see how you were. I'm amazed that you are still with us.'

He wished me well and left. It wasn't until then I realised just how serious the whole situation was and, yes, yet again I could have died. As Mum would suggest, it wasn't my time, and still someone had been looking down on me from the age of six, when I should have drowned.

After rehabilitation, I started to gain my strength, bringing up my girls as best I could. In winter 1995, I took them on holiday to Mauritius. Mum and Dad would join us a day later.

The holiday complex was beautiful and perfect, with many individual sea-facing apartments and villas dotted around, overlooking a fringed palm beach. We were the first to arrive and told that many others were expected to fill up the complex by the end of the week. Whilst I was airing the place and settling in, my girls ran around playing hide and seek in between the empty apartments. I kept telling them to not do so, and explained others were due to arrive, but kids being kids, they rarely took notice and would continue playing.

That same afternoon, there was a knock at the door. A middle-aged lady was standing with Arlena, speaking in English. 'Is this your child? I found her running on our veranda next door.'

I apologised and told her that she had been doing this all morning, but she laughed and didn't seem to mind. I thanked her for bringing her back. She introduced herself and told me that she was expecting her family to arrive from South Africa and Australia. Assuming I was English because of my accent and my dyed blonde hair, she asked where I lived in England. I told her I was actually Mauritian. Taken aback, she commented that I didn't look typically Mauritian. She asked for my family name.

When I told her, she replied, 'I knew someone with that surname. She was called Danielle.'

I replied, 'That's my name!'

She looked at me as though she'd seen a ghost, with one hand over her mouth in total disbelief.

I was puzzled at her reaction, she stood back and said, 'I'm Michelle. Don't you remember me? I was the lady who tried to adopt you at the convent.'

I stood there in recollection, as tears filled my eyes, I too was stunned! I thought, *what are the odds?* We sat on the veranda and talked as though there was no tomorrow. She held my hands tightly, giving my girls the impression she was a family member.

She said, 'Robert will have a shock when I tell him.'

She then made the suggestion that we should surprise him, which I thought would be fantastic. Later that evening, Robert turned up with Michelle, and as expected his reaction was the same. When Mum and Dad arrived, I couldn't wait to tell them the news. Their silence gave away that they weren't happy. Given the circumstances, I guess they didn't want to be judged too harshly.

We spent a few weeks on the complex and used every opportunity to spend as much time together as possible. Their extended family became aware of our history and welcomed me with open arms. Christiane was her sister-in-law, who lived in South Africa. From the outset, she proved to be an amazing character. We gelled straight away. She was great fun to be around and made my holiday even more pleasurable. We continue to remain friends, and have often taken turns to visit each other in the UK, South Africa and even met up once or twice back home in Mauritius.

Being a single mum meant I didn't venture out much socially. On one of those rare occasions, at a friend's barbecue I was introduced to Sharon. From the minute I met her, I knew we'd be friends. We were similar in so many ways, and somehow each knew what the other was thinking, acting as though we'd known each other for years. She was also a single mum of three. Our kids would play together, and we became inseparable, seeing each other through good and bad times. Sharon has been in my life for nearly thirty years, and I can honestly say she is my best friend.

# Chapter 13
## The One

Growing up, Arlena was quiet and shy, rarely demanding any attention. Being a healthy child made it easy to care for her. She was always glued to the TV, watching cartoons. Along with many others, her favourite show was *My Wife and Kids*. She'd watch these to a point that enabled her to mimic the characters, which would kill me with laughter. She also had a natural talent when it came to dance. Without any formal training whatsoever, she won a dancing competition at the age of three. Realising these talents, I enrolled both Arlena and Zoyla in dance and drama school to help with their development.

In 1995, whilst at a birthday celebration, a mutual friend introduced me to Mark. He was seven years younger than me, but looked older, coming across as well educated in the way he spoke and presented himself. I learnt that he worked for a local racing team. He never married or had children of his own. It wasn't his good looks or sporty physique that caught my attention, but his humorous side that attracted me the most. Enjoying a few hours of laughter and getting to know each other was as far as it got that night.

A few weeks later, I received a call from him. He had got my number from the same friend. I agreed to meet him for a drink, which became two and so on. From then on, our time together felt natural and effortless; we simply enjoyed each other's company. I wouldn't introduce him to my girls until much later. I let my guard down enough to allow him to know the real me. The more we saw each other, the more intense our love became. There, I said it: that magical word, love. It's true what they say: it comes when you least expect it. At the age of thirty-seven, I finally found The One. The love between us was real.

What was different? A feeling that I couldn't put my finger on. I simply loved spending time with him. He made no demands and up until he met me, he was leading a playboy lifestyle, which he was happy to leave behind. He was an eligible bachelor, with a desirable job, owned his own property and was financially stable – although I didn't share his passion for cricket, which would take him away on various tours.

My girls eventually met him, and loved having him around, after which Mark naturally formed part of our lives. We enjoyed family holidays together and sometimes he'd whisk me off to distant shores, treating me like a queen. Over the years, many men have tried to make me feel special, but Mark didn't need to; I felt special being around him. I made it clear from the outset that marriage would never be on the cards, and nor could I ever give him a child, which he didn't mind. He simply wanted me and wasn't going anywhere, constantly demonstrating his undying love for me.

Sharon had met Dean, and as couples we'd spend some memorable evenings together. Mark also shared my passion for hosting dinner parties, which we did on many occasions. He was similar to Dad in the way that he'd make sure your glass was never empty. The family became aware that I was in love with this man and welcomed him. Being an only child made him appreciate our large family.

He once helped me build a Coco Loco Beach Bar, which went down well at Jean Marc's 40th birthday celebration. It was fancy dress, and the theme was typically Mauritian. It would give Mark a taste of our culture, which he found truly amazing, and wanted to know more about. We often talked about going there for one of our getaways.

It was now time for me to meet his parents. As it turned out, I was to be the first woman he had ever introduced to them.

Driving towards the coast down south, I wanted to know all there was about his family. His dad was a retired army sergeant and a golf enthusiast, his mum was a retired doctor and a keen gardener. Mark hadn't told them much about me, which made me even more nervous, thoughts running through my mind, like, *what if they don't like me? Or judge me for having been married twice, with two children from two fathers?* I knew there was nothing to be ashamed of, especially when it came to my children, but unfortunately, not everybody sees the true picture.

People can be so judgemental, but Mark, being Mark, would say, 'All will be fine. If I love you, they'll love you, too.'

Reassured by this, I was able to breathe a bit more. Driving through the pretty coastal town of Totnes, we eventually pulled up into their drive. The cottage was picture postcard. My reaction was, 'Wow!'

Mark said, 'I'll show you the River Dart, which runs at the back. It's my favourite place ever.'

Shaking with anxiety as we walked on the gravel, I didn't know what to expect. His mum was standing at the front door waiting to welcome us.

Mark greeted her with, 'All right, Janet?' which I thought was odd, no kisses or anything. I had taken a bunch of flowers, which I presented to her at the door, before reaching to give her a kiss on the cheeks. Her body language gave away that she wasn't accustomed to it, but she went with it anyway.

Walking through the long corridor gave away that they were incredibly upper-middle-class, judging purely by the furniture and décor, at which point, I had a déjà vu moment. 'I've been here before.'

I recognised the setting, standing exactly where I was, and hearing the exact words. I hadn't had a moment like that since leaving Mauritius. The feeling was so real, something that still baffles me to this day.

We went into the lounge, where his dad was sat reading a paper. He got up and formally shook Mark's hands, which naturally made me do the same, but he pulled me towards him, giving me a hug, saying, 'She's a beauty, Mark!'

My thoughts were, *surely, you'd say that about a horse!* His mum disappeared into the kitchen before re-entering, carrying a large tray containing her best china that she placed on the coffee table. The whole setting seemed formal, which didn't make me feel at ease.

The conversation was a little dry. I didn't share their interest in gardening or golf. The men spoke mainly about cricket. After tea, his mum gave me a tour of the garden, which I had to pretend I was interested in. Although it looked pretty, I couldn't begin to repeat the names she was giving to all her plants. I patiently wandered around with her, then came the subject of my work, family etc., I told her all that Mark should have. She didn't say much after that.

After spending a couple of hours with them, I got the impression Mark was keen to leave. On our way back, he tried to tell me that they liked me, but I wasn't convinced. I also got the impression that although grateful for his family, he wasn't necessarily close to them. It seems his dad's job took him overseas a lot, which was why Mark was sent to boarding school, and possibly the reason for the lack of intimacy between them and why Mark rarely visited them.

Mark and I travelled to many destinations. One of the most memorable was a holiday to the Dominican Republic. It was truly amazing, until he suffered a bout of sunstroke. During his recovery, he felt terrible for possibly ruining our time together. One day I left him to sleep it off, whilst I went down to sunbathe. A few hours later, I arrived back in the room. Mark had champagne on the ready and was holding something in the palm of his hands. It was a ring, shaped like a globe. This unique, three-in-one, sphere-shaped ring had small hinges on the side, which allowed it to be rotated and worn in multiple ways, as in engagement, wedding or eternity ring.

Mark uttered the following: 'I know, you said that you don't want to marry, but this ring is shaped in the way I feel for you. Yes, I think the world of you.'

I looked at him in awe, scared at what was coming next.

Rotating the bands, he continued, 'In case you change your mind and we are engaged, you can wear it this way' – he rotated the bands –'or if you want to marry me, you can then wear it this way' – finally this all-in-one piece of jewellery came together – 'but for now, I want you to wear it as an eternity ring.'

His words rang true and melted me inside, and I could have quite easily said yes, but I chose to capture the moment and it is one that will remain etched in my memory until I die.

Naturally, I wanted it to be perfect with Mark. Valuing what we had, I didn't want to lose this perfect guy. A few years later, we both felt it was time for us to live together. The girls were also happy to do this. With our properties on the market, mine sold immediately, and I found us the perfect house, with the girls' school right opposite. When it was time for us to complete, Mark decided that he'd buy the place without my financial input, but expected us to still move in with him. I was staggered by the way he duped me. I instantly knew this lack of trust would destroy us.

I needed to understand what changed. It turned out his family, friends and lawyers advised him to go it alone, given the fact that the children weren't his, making him vulnerable if it all went pear-shaped between us. He was always aware that I had walked out of two marriages without taking so much as a penny. Did he really think that it was his roof that I needed, or what I could financially gain from him? What happened to the love he felt for me? He was so wrong about me – or was he? Did I really value myself so highly? What made me think I was perfect?

If there were any flaws on my part, he'd never tell me, but would hope that I'd recognise these before it was too late.

Unfortunately, I wasn't perfect. In reality, I was already damaged goods, trying to repair myself after each failed relationship. Like every broken thing of value, the beauty is there, but the cracks become more noticeable if not properly mended.

It's true to say I had high expectations of others. Having seen how the men in my family treat their loved ones led me to expect to be valued and treated the same way. Up until then, Mark seemed perfect in every way, and was the only man that gave me the love and respect I craved throughout my life. This might have been the reason why I held on a little too tight, so as not to lose what we had, but in doing so my behaviour flagged up many red lights.

My past experiences would dominate my behaviour towards others. In short, consider the traumatic treatment whilst living in the convent, the abusive marriage, the lies and deceit by others who saw me as vulnerable, all of which undoubtedly had a negative impact that would lead me to be the person I became. In order to survive, rightly or wrongly, I learnt to control my emotions, and carefully chose who I'd give my time to, and would further detach myself from those I resented for hurting me. It's true I walked out of many relationships, and based purely on this I believe Mark thought I would do the same to him.

Finally, having to cope and succeed as a single parent, I needed to have a routine and structure in place. Meals and bedtimes were regularly scheduled. Focusing on my children's safety and finances enabled the smooth running of our household. I wanted everything to be perfect, and, more importantly, I didn't want to fail my girls. However, some of these factors may have meant I came across as controlling, but I saw it more as having everything under control. Of course, if Mark felt I was a bit controlling he never picked me up on it. If only he had, things might have been different between us.

As expected, the lack of trust on my part caused a wedge between us, I questioned his loyalty, but my love for him allowed me to continue seeing him. Unlike previous relationships, I found it difficult to simply walk away. Refusing to jeopardise my girls' security, I showed Mark that I didn't need his house, and decided to rent a small cottage so we'd never be left out in the cold.

With an increase in rent, I later moved into a three-bedroom house that was cheaper, and closer to the girls' secondary school. Once I felt the girls had settled in their new school and needed less of my attention, I was able to help Mum decorate her cakes. Her health hadn't improved, which was impaired by being diabetic. I took great joy in decorating cakes, which led me to master the skill and enrol on a course in the art of sugar flowers. After I qualified, Mum was thrilled at my newfound skill, which made all the difference to her finished cakes, enabling her to sell these at a better profit.

After 9/11, flights were on the cheap. It seemed no one wanted to travel. Bernard, being the generous one, treated us all to a family holiday to Cyprus, and twenty-two of us had an amazing time, one of the best times ever spent as a family.

Unfortunately, Dad became ill. On his return to England and after seeing a specialist, we received the dreadful news that he had throat cancer, and didn't have long to live. You can imagine our devastation. Having surgery to remove his tongue would allow him extra time with us. It was barbaric, to say the least.

The sad news overshadowed us all as a family. I was now going through early menopause, on top of which I received a diagnosis of rheumatoid osteoporosis picked up after an MRI result for two slipped discs. My health wasn't the best. The menopause alone came with its own challenges. I didn't really know what to expect, but there were clear signs of physical and emotional changes going on, initially showing in my lack of patience. I became short-tempered, I stopped feeling desirable and gained weight for no reason, all of which added to the pressures of being a parent and was affecting my relationship with Mark. We were arguing more, mainly because I was nit-picking on anything and everything.

Unbeknown to me, those changes also caused me to act differently towards my closest friends. I was like a she-devil, a side that I didn't recognise. In fact, it brought the worst out of me. I questioned everything, which made me appear jealous, especially when I received a phone call whilst at Mark's place.

The phone rang, and a female voice in a foreign accent asked to speak to Mark, but he was out. She seemed surprised on hearing another woman's voice.

In poor English, she said, 'I caw from Thailand. Wish Mark Happy Valentine.'

I asked, 'Who's this?'

She replied, 'I his girlfren' from Thailand. I wish him Happy Valentine. And you, who you?'

In my anger, I sternly replied, 'I'm his wife and he has six kids.'

Her response was, 'Oh Mark maweed – oh!'

With all my anger, I slammed the receiver down. She didn't call back. Would you have done the same? I felt terrible for lying, but I was fuming and torn inside out! My world was crumbling around me. I wanted to walk out there and then, but I needed Mark to see how he hurt me, so I waited for his return and confronted him with it.

His reply was, 'She's just a friend I met on the last holidays with the lads. It's over with now.'

I hoped this holiday had been before he met me, and as it turned out, it was a few months beforehand.

I must have expressed a certain amount of jealousy, which would at times have brought out the ugly side of me, but the emotions were raw. With alarm bells ringing, of course, I became suspicious of him, after which the relationship between us was on and off. The last straw was finding an expensive-looking piece of women's jewellery at the back of the sofa that didn't belong to any of us. This elevated my suspicion that he'd had another affair. I decided to confront him with it, and he didn't deny it, but simply took the jewellery from me. What would you have done?

We had booked to go to Mauritius later that year. Despite the fact that I still loved him, my suspicion was eating away at me, the thought that he had been unfaithful, and nor did I ever get over the fact that he jeopardised mine and my children's security, which left me unable to obtain a mortgage. This, together with the thought that he had it in him to hurt me, finally gave me the strength to leave him. He wasn't that perfect after all. I stopped beating myself up about my negative behaviour that made me appear in the wrong, when in fact, Mark was aware of his own weaknesses that would potentially end what we had. Which is why he bought the house on his own, because he simply didn't trust himself.

On top of this, it was the saddest time of my life, watching Dad suffering without the use of his tongue, which took away all that he enjoyed, food, drink and telling jokes. He wasn't the same person. I spent a lot of time with him during his last months and helped care for him. However, he lost the fight in the winter of 2002.

After that, Mark came to see me. He suggested that I could do with a break and we should still go on holiday to Mauritius, which I agreed with. Although we still had strong feelings for each other, in some way we had drifted apart. Being there reminded me of Dad, especially seeing his younger brother Hervais, who was his double. I can't say the holiday was the best we had.

Losing Dad broke my heart, and I knew Mark and I were history. The only way I could survive the terrible feeling was to detach myself emotionally. The practice I had over the years would make this easier. I hoped that Mark would marry and have children of his own. After we separated, I would never see him again. Seventeen years on, I remain single to this day, comforted only with the feeling that I was once loved – but life goes on.

I focused on working voluntarily with the witness service at the Crown Court, which was rewarding. It also opened up an opportunity for me to work at the same court as an usher. Being a single mum, working full time and juggling two teenage girls didn't always come without its challenges. I tried to achieve a balance in the way I brought my girls up, but there were times when I would lay down some rules, which sometimes come across as me being strict, but what parent doesn't have rules and discipline their child to an extent? At the age of fifteen, Zoyla decided to live with her dad. It didn't come as a surprise. Deep down I knew she'd been hurt in some way. If she was unhappy, I'd never know the real reasons why. For personal reasons, I write very little about her, but she remains a big part of me.

When I turned fifty, I remember having a conversation with Arlena about reaching this age and thinking that there's got to be more to life, so I came up with the idea that would bring some adventure into my life. Up to now, all I'd experienced was drama. I wasn't going to wait for things to happen, but more, *I'm going to make it happen!* Without planning, I was going to use the next opportunity that showed itself. That same weekend, *Big Brother* auditions were being advertised on TV.

Arlena piped up with, 'There you go, Mum, there's your opportunity. I dare you to audition.'

I was always up for a dare, and rarely took myself seriously, so naturally I went for it. It was a Sunday. Arlena and I drove up to Birmingham, where we stood in line for hours, before it was my turn to audition along with hundreds of eighteen to thirty-year-olds. I couldn't believe they took an interest long enough to see me through to the third round. I didn't get much further than that, but the experience was fun.

That same year, I signed up to *CelebAir*, where I was chosen to take part as a passenger on a flight to Faro, with a host of celebrities acting as 'trolley dollies', including Chico, Mica Paris and Tamara Beckwith. Arlena, my ex-sister-in-law and I travelled on an all-expenses-paid trip for taking part. It was hilarious and a great experience.

This final act was for a bit of spotlight. I applied to appear on *GMTV* for a hair makeover with Charles Worthington. I sent in my worst picture of a bad hair day and I was chosen to feature on the show. Meeting Fern Britton and Phillip Schofield was an experience in itself. When it came to the style, I wasn't allowed to see what was being done until it was over. The reveal was aired live. Words weren't necessary as my face said it all, after which I stopped putting myself out there, thinking: *no more risks*. However, being the unbridled character that I am, I rarely say no to a bit of good clean fun.

# Chapter 14
# New Challenges

Being resourceful, I made the most of what we had to keep our heads above water, at the same time trying to be positive; it wasn't always easy to deal with some of the challenges that we have no control over. Arlena hated school, I'll never know the extent of the bullying that went on, which clearly affected her. However, she excelled in dance and enjoyed horse riding, with just one or two friends. She rarely ventured out. Although shy and timid, you couldn't miss the bright spark in her eyes. Everyone recognised her beauty and she was naturally photogenic. I tried to help bring her out of her shell by encouraging her to take up modelling in the hope that it would give her some confidence. After numerous applications, Arlena was finally accepted by a reputable agency, who offered her some modelling work. Her ability to dance gave her an opportunity to feature in a music video, but although she found it fun, her heart and soul wasn't in it.

As mentioned, she was a healthy child, but one summer she woke up with an unusually high temperature. A doctor checked her body for a rash, and it turned out to be nothing but a common cold, but pointed out that she had idiopathic scoliosis. He showed me the obvious curve on her back, something I hadn't noticed up until that point, and nor did she ever complain of any pain. My initial thoughts were that it might have been caused through dance or horse riding, but the doctor said that the condition was probably something she was born with, and wouldn't become apparent until there was a growth spurt in adolescence. Naturally, we were worried about how this could affect her in later life. After a referral to see a specialist in Oxford, we were given various options. Initially, she would have to wear a body brace specially made for her, in the hope that it would stop the curve from getting worse, which could potentially develop into severe spinal deformity. For the next nine months we travelled back and forth to Oxford where she was continually being monitored, but without any change. It was agreed that she'd have corrective surgery, which meant a spinal fusion, leaving her with permanent rods in her back.

Arlena's hope of a career as a professional dancer was shattered. Over the following years, I'd try to encourage her to continue with dance, but she had lost interest and confidence. After surgery, I felt even more protective of her. Her recovery was slow, meaning less time at school and interacting with friends, which didn't help with her self-esteem.

Once she had fully recovered, she went to college to study drama. Initially, she stayed at her dad's place because it was easier for her to travel back and forth to college, but she rarely came home. I got the feeling he allowed her more freedom. As it turned out, she had met a young boy named Cameron who was on the same course. She was smitten with him, but I wasn't to know about this until months later. Seeing her at my nephew's wedding, although very beautiful, her behaviour had changed. She seemed distant and certainly a different person from the one I was used to. It was then that I learnt about Cameron, who in my opinion was clearly the influence behind the change in her. Naturally, I didn't approve, and held him responsible for taking away the spark from my daughter's life.

Until that point, I lived purely for my girls. Their absence left a void that was hard to cope with. I tried to enjoy the freedom of not having to cook, clean and tidy up after them, but in reality I missed doing all of those things. I was feeling abandoned, undervalued, unworthy and unloved. It was no one's fault. I had chosen to live this way, but I can't say I was totally happy. I still missed Mark, but deep down I knew we could never be together, a fact that I came to accept.

Since losing Dad, Mum tried to move on with her life as best as she could. However, her health deteriorated, which resulted in a leg amputation. Being in a wheelchair limited her in so many ways. Her love for baking had to stop. It was clearly what kept her going for so long, after which life was never the same. She survived a few more years, and, like Dad, she suffered terribly before passing away. We all grieved the loss in different ways and some coped better than others. Being a large family with many opinions, there were sure to be disagreements on how the final arrangements should be handled, causing some to butt heads, making the devastating situation more stressful, not always ideal in the raw emotions of the mourning process.

Many of us will agree Mum and Dad were the glue that bonded us as a family. This became obvious when we started seeing less and less of one another. Family gatherings were never the same. I cherish having Jacqueline close to me and I hold her dear. It would see the odd few like Eric, Gert, myself and Shirley to organise family gatherings, but the attempts for us to reunite became tiresome. These days, the only time you can guarantee we'd all be together is at a funeral, which is sad. I'd rather hope that some would make more of an effort whilst you are still breathing. I can't imagine what Mum and Dad would make of it all. I am the first to admit that I detached myself at the time, choosing to step away as a coping mechanism to avoid further emotional upsets. Perhaps unknowingly, some of my siblings were doing the same.

Mum's gift of cake-making was passed on to me. I decided to run my own cake business, alongside working full time at the courthouse. Although a secure job, I found myself working alongside colleagues that were not very friendly, and some would go out of their way to make life difficult. I'm sure many have experienced irritating individuals in the workplace, but have been limited to what they could do about it. For a number of years, I put up with it. Detachment or simply stepping away was not ideal in this situation. I needed to pay the bills, and hoped things would improve.

A few years later, I became aware that Creole interpreters were being sought after to deal with a great number of Chagossians arriving in the UK. After many years of campaigning to return to their homeland, an alteration to the law in Britain enabled descendants born in British Indian Ocean Territory (BIOT) to register as British citizens, meaning any Chagossians exiled from their homeland together with their second and possibly third-generation family were now able to obtain a British passport. Those who could afford the plane fare took up the opportunity and found themselves in Crawley, a small market town in Sussex, England.

Naturally, my rare language skill allowed me to embrace the opportunity and I enrolled on a course to achieve the required qualification of Diploma in Public Service Interpreting, focusing on the aspect of law. This in turn enabled me to register with various agencies and governmental bodies such as the Home Office.

These jobs would find me travelling the length and breadth of the country. Unfortunately, I hated driving long distances, especially to areas that I wasn't familiar with, which led me to travel mainly by train. It was then that I adopted the nickname Choo Choo!

My years of working in the criminal courts system, together with not having the children living at home, gave me the confidence and freedom to take on the role of freelance interpreter. I left the court to take on assignments to assist various governmental bodies in their functions, dealing with crime, family and immigration issues. The job was intense, but proved to be one of the most interesting and rewarding that I've ever been involved in.

Although I didn't see my girls as often, I never stopped worrying about them. Arlena introduced me to Cameron, who was equally in love with her, but I had my reservations and would at times voice this. He needed to prove that he was deserving of her. I will admit I didn't make it easy for him, but soon realised his qualities. I loved his confidence and intelligence. He had a certain way about him and was naturally talented when it came to acting and singing. His quirky sense of humour made him all the more fun to be around, so after a time I learnt to respect him, because he did make Arlena happy.

The house was empty and too big for one person. I downsized to a bungalow and moved to a remote village away from it all, initially loving the peace and the country air, but within six months I started to feel cut off from the world.

It was May 2017 when Arlena and Cameron had come to stay for a short break. Arlena's natural love of animals came from living with her dad, whose girlfriend worked at the local vet's. She'd tell me stories of rescued animals that would be brought home from there, so it was no surprise to see them with a dog of their own, a little Yorkshire terrier named Jasper. He was tiny, playful and yapped a lot, and was their joy in life. Personally, I was never one for animals, but after a short time and seeing the way he'd show you love and affection, it didn't take me long to simply adore him.

One morning I took him for a walk whilst going to vote at the village hall. On our way back, three sheepdogs belonging to a local farmer were left in an open-top Jeep. After clocking Jasper, all three decided to jump out the back of this vehicle, and within seconds began chasing him into a nearby field, in an attempt to attack him. I was still holding on to the lead. Unable to get them off and hearing Jasper squeal sent shivers down my back. I feared the worst. I was shaking whilst trying to rein him in. He was now closer, but I couldn't pick him up because the dogs were nipping at my hands and ankles. Jasper ran from them making it even more difficult to get hold of him.

On hearing the commotion, the farmer came out, unable to command his dogs. I kept shouting for him to help, and he eventually managed to get hold of Jasper and handed him over to me. I could see he was bleeding, but didn't know how badly hurt he was. I held him tightly and started to run.

A neighbour standing at his gate shouted out, 'They're coming after you!' which didn't help.

Without looking back, I ran for dear life with the dogs in pursuit. Arriving at the house, I banged on the door and fell in the hallway. Jasper was motionless, which gave the impression he was dead, I worried that Arlena and Cameron would blame me for their loss.

Jasper suffered multiple puncture wounds and was clearly in shock. The farmer had no qualms with paying the £450 vet's bill. This was an experience that would affect me for years to come. After they left, I was afraid to go outdoors, for fear of seeing these dogs that lived close by, causing me to isolate myself. It wasn't long before the depression set in. I started drinking more and more alcohol. Although it was only wine, it got to the point where I would go through five bottles a week. To some, it may not seem that much, but combined with medication and health issues, this didn't help. The trauma of it all affected me terribly, and I lived this way for a year without making my family aware, not even my closest friends.

I wasn't proud of myself. I was drinking to fill the void in my life. Secluding myself was easy, as hardly anyone came to visit; the distance and location had put people off visiting on a regular basis. I can't blame anyone for my lifestyle, but I knew that I had lost the will to live. In the realisation that I was just existing and not living, I'd lost my way somehow, with no purpose in life. The only thing I was certain of was that death would come, so why wait for the inevitable?

The weakness in me wanted it to happen sooner. Yes, I'm ashamed to say I tried to end my life with alcohol and pills. Being a coward, I didn't want it to be painful, I just wanted to go to sleep and not wake up. I didn't feel I had anyone to talk to, and nor did I think anyone cared enough to listen. When the deed was done, I woke in the night with excruciating abdominal pain, never realising that I was going to feel this bad; after all, I was taking painkillers. Unable to bear with the pain, I found myself in A&E where they showed no mercy. Who can blame them? I woke up the next morning feeling ashamed, with Mum's words echoing in my ears. She'd say, 'Taking one's own life is the biggest sin you can ever commit.'

I had visits from doctors, the mental health team and I'm sure an officer had questioned me at some point, all looking to understand why I made this attempt. Before I was released from hospital, I was allocated a mental health worker. I didn't feel I deserved their attention and just wanted to leave the hospital because I felt shameful.

I dreamt of Mum that evening and woke up needing to find a church, to confess, as it laid heavily on my conscience. I had turned my back on my religion for some time; I didn't even know where my local church was. After a few enquiries, I eventually found it and met the most amazing priest known as Canon Brendan Kileen (but most knew him as  Father Brendan) who heard my confession, but he didn't just stop there. He wanted to know how I got to this point. He patiently listened to my reasons for wanting to disappear, but he had other ideas. He made arrangements for me to spend some time in Turvey Abbey, Bedfordshire. I found myself living there for a week, without any communication with the outside world, no TV, mobile or even a newspaper. I was living a simple life within a religious environment. Whilst there, I spent every day praying in the chapel, carrying out simple duties to help the community, with some meditation in the evenings, all of which filled me with love and peace. I prayed for the will to live and help with my drinking. I knew that I needed to stop the habit if I was to survive the year. This would be my next challenge. I didn't know how to or whether I wanted to give up completely because I enjoyed it too much, but at the same time it was poisoning me.

On leaving the abbey, I felt different and a change in the way I valued my life, which made me want to protect it even more. Both my girls had moved on with their lives, living with their partners. Cameron and Arlena's love for one another was undeniable. He was genuinely a good man and certainly proved to be patient, especially when it came to me. My respect for him was elevated after he asked me for Arlena's hand in marriage. Unfortunately, I never got to know his family as well. His dad lived abroad and he had lost his mum soon after. I know she'd be proud of him.

A few months later, an announcement came that I was to be a grandma. The excitement filled me with joy. I also found myself at my niece's baby shower, talking to a group of ladies. One in particular was boasting about how she gave up the drink. I must admit I was envious, and needed to understand how she was so calm around a table full of wine bottles.

I had to ask the question, 'How did you manage it?'

She simply replied, 'I read a book.'

But that didn't explain it to me. I couldn't believe that reading a book was all it took. Of course, I was curious and needed to know more. I made a note of the title and author: *The Easy Way for Women to Stop Drinking* by Allen Carr. I didn't intend to buy this straight away, but a few weeks later whilst browsing in a charity shop, I came across the very book, staring back at me from the shelf. I had to pick it up. *50p*, I thought. *Why not?* Within the first twenty minutes of reading through it, I knew that I'd never want to drink again and that's how simple it was for me, too. I can't explain it, it was like magic. It felt as though I was brainwashed, but only time would tell. It's been over three years and I'm still not missing the wine.

I wanted to be the perfect grandma, because I never knew or spent quality time with my grandparents, something I felt was missing throughout my life. It was also important for me to be sober, so my time with my grandchildren would be meaningful.

The mental health team tried to help me overcome my fears of leaving the house, but although they helped in some way with the depression, I continue to struggle seeing dogs, even on their leads. It's an issue that I'm still having to deal with. The only dog I feel safe around is Jasper. When I'm out, I would carefully choose places I visit; the park is definitely not one of them.

That same year I had the pleasure of meeting one of Jacqueline's friends named Dominica. Everybody needs a Dom in their lives, as she is simply the most easy-going person ever, and one of the most loyal. Being of foreign descent, Dom understands our family values, which made us grow closer over a period of time and, like Sharon, she's always there for me.

The book completely changed my life for the better. It allowed me to focus on a new way of life, bringing a balance to my health and finances. I started to look and feel more like myself, enjoying a more active social life with friends. I had been given a second chance in life. Up until that dreadful night, I rarely went to church. I now go regularly, and seeing Father Branden at the altar always brings comfort to me. He always gives me an assuring smile, and I believe he is always happy to see that I am doing well which I'm sure comforted him too. He advised me to go on a retreat with the church to Medjugorje in Croatia. It was the most amazing experience, a place where I felt reborn again, ready for the next chapter in my life.

A year later, I moved closer to my family, which made all the difference. I learnt to love my space and my own company, whilst choosing to associate only with family and my closest friends, who have been longstanding. I hold them dear, because there's never any awkwardness. We share a good level of communication and our relationship flows naturally. They are truly amazing and bring enough joy and love to last me a lifetime.

However, it wasn't always so, because there was a time when I felt I couldn't even speak to them about my difficulties. I felt I needed to detach myself and become unavailable, not because I didn't value them in any way, but purely because I didn't want them to see the ugly side of my being. My depression brought out the worst in me, so, again, I feared being judged in some way, or maybe, I thought they, too, would want to detach from me for bringing drama into their lives. *If I was able to do this, why can't they?* was the way I was thinking.

My negative vibes were not something I was always proud of. Many have said if they were true friends, they would have been there for you, but I feared losing them in the process. In the end, my true friends remained true to me, so I thank Sharon, Dom, Christiane, Theresa, Joy, Rosa, Leylo and Ann for all your patience. Each one holds an amazing quality that I admire. Thank you for bearing with me. I also consider Arlena and my youngest sister Jacqueline to be my best friends. I don't know what I'd do without them.

# Chapter 15
# A Never-ending Struggle

Once the Chagossians community in the UK was formed, many found it difficult to settle here due to the pressure of being separated from their extended family. Before arriving in the UK, many were already suffering depression from the effects of the expulsion from their homeland. The lack of English didn't help with employment and housing. They faced a different kind of racism during their settlement, which added to their never-ending struggle.

Working as an interpreter exposes you to a lot of vulnerable situations where you see and feel people's misery and pain. The job expects you to be impartial in controlling your feelings and personal views. Dealing with refugees is probably the toughest, as I can relate to their struggles in coping and living in a new land. Watching children unsure of their future leads me to think of our own struggles as a family when we arrived in the UK. Now I am faced with watching young children struggling when being removed from their families, or some who cannot go home and placed in an institution, to begin an uncertain journey and possibly more pain and struggles.

Having worked alongside many Chagossians over the years, I too took an interest in their fight for justice and wanted to know how realistic it was for them to finally return to their homeland. After contacting my local MP on the subject, the following letter was a response from the House of Commons, which I thought may explain the British Government's views on the subject.

Rt Hon. Andrea Leadsom MP
House of Commons
London
SW1A 0AA
www.gov.uk/fcdo
05 October 2021

Dear Andrea,

Thank you for your correspondence of 27 August to the former Foreign Secretary, on behalf of your constituent Ms Danielle Staples about Chagossians and the British Indian Territory Islands (BIOT). I am replying as the Minister for the Overseas Territories.

The UK Government has expressed sincere regret about the manner in which Chagossians were removed from BIOT in the 1960s and 1970s. Substantial compensation (around £15.5 million in current prices) has been paid to Chagossians since the time of their removal. British courts and the European Court of Human Rights have confirmed that compensation has been paid in full and final settlement. The Ilois Trust Fund was also established in the early 1980s to disburse an extra-gratia UK payment of £4m to the Government of Mauritius on behalf of Chagossians there. The bulk of the expenditure was cash payments or housing construction. The British Overseas Territories Act 2002 granted the right to British citizenship to British Overseas Territories citizens, including a large number of Chagossians, giving them a right of abode in the UK.

The UK has no doubt about its sovereignty over the Chagos Archipelago, which has been under continuous British sovereignty since 1814. Mauritius has never held sovereignty over the Archipelago and we do not recognise its claim. However, we have a long standing commitment, first made in 1965, to cede sovereignty of the territory to Mauritius when it is no longer required for defence purposes. We stand by that commitment.

In November 2016, the UK Government announced that resettlement of Chagossians could not be supported on the grounds of feasibility, defence and security interests, and cost to the British taxpayer. The decision not to support resettlement followed an independent feasibility study of the practicalities of resettlement (published in February 2015) and a public consultation (results published in January 2016).

While it has decided not to support resettlement, the UK Government is determined to address the aspirations of Chagossians which made them seek to resettle; the desire for better lives, and to maintain a connection to the Territory. In order to meet those aspirations, the UK Government announced in November 2016 that it would implement a support package worth approximately £40m over ten years. The support package intends to provide Chagossians in the communities in which they currently live -

predominantly UK, Mauritius and Seychelles - with better life chances demonstrating our commitment to minority ethnic groups. Support will focus on improved access to health and social care, better education and employment opportunities, and cultural conservation.

In Mauritius, the Support Package has been funding English language courses for the Chagossian community. Since 2019, 217 Chagossians have participated in these courses run by the British Council. More English language and Business Skills courses will be delivered in the coming months.

In the United Kingdom, the FCDO advertised a Call for Bids in October 2020, inviting organisations to bid for funding from the Support Package to deliver projects that will benefit the Chagossian community. This resulted in FCDO signing Grant Agreements with three charitable organisations which seek to support the Chagossian community in the UK. In November 2020 the FCDO signed contracts with Crawley College, to provide English language courses, and with the UK National Information Centre for the recognition and evaluation of international qualifications and skills (UK ENIC) for the provision of statements of comparability for qualifications that have been gained outside of the UK.

Another element of the Support Package is to enable Chagossians wherever they may live to maintain a connection with the Territory through a more frequent programme of visits to BIOT. Eight heritage visits have taken place since November 2017, with 154 Chagossians each spending a week visiting the Territory. The visits were well received by those participating, and more visits will take place in the future. Unfortunately, however, heritage visits to BIOT have been suspended since March 2020 due to the COVID-19 pandemic. The FCDO is absolutely committed to progressing the programme as and when it is safe to do so.

Yours sincerely
Minister for Overseas Territories

I felt very despondent and reflected on people's life struggles, and how they find themselves there. I asked myself, *how do we stop the pain and aim for a better outcome?* I often wondered whether my friend Ursulle, whose husband may have been from the Chagos Island, and therefore, was entitled to settle in the UK. I'd like to think they're already here and living a better life with their son. Who knows, will I ever see her again?

Focusing on my own struggles and suffering, it dawned on me that it didn't destroy me, but defined who I became.

Mentally, I can honestly say, I'm in a better place. I enjoy living a calm, simple and uncomplicated life, and don't expect too much from it. Happy that both my girls are settled, I no longer feel that I need to live for them. Detachment is a tool I use as a coping mechanism to survive, where no medication or therapy is required. Some of you may feel that living a life without a man to love is a waste, but in reality, it's been proven that I am a happier person alone. Perhaps you're thinking, surely it can't be good for someone to emotionally detach themselves from others. You could even suggest that numbing yourself to emotions and feelings may be unhealthy, for it can be seen as an inability to show empathy or a fear of commitment.

For me, emotional detachment is my way of coping with overwhelming people, activities and situations. In that sense, it can be healthy because I get to choose when to be involved or when to step away. Some readers will identify with this behaviour. It may not be for everyone, but it works for me.

If you are reading this book and can recognise yourself in some way, I urge you to be reassured that it is possible to achieve what appears to be impossible. Just have faith that it can happen. I'm a great believer that fate plays a big part in all our lives; I'm living proof of that. I believe that the way I overcame my depression and drinking habits was to go so far down the path until it was a case of sink or swim. As Mum would say, 'It's not your time.' I pray the time that I have been given is proving positive to someone out there, even if I can't see it.

Further details on the Chagossians' fight for justice can be found here:

www.una.org.uk/magazine/2018-1/fifty-years-fighting-better-futur

www.chagossupport.org.uk/chagossian-struggle-in-the-media

# Epilogue

Through this book, I'll be leaving the legacy of my memory bank to the next generation in our family and to my grandchildren, who may never meet and get to know me. This book will tell them all they need understand about their roots, and one they should never forget. As well as the UK, Mauritius is a wonderful country with just as much mystery in its colourful history. I would encourage them to use skills that they possess and learn all there is to know. knowledge is the key that I didn't possess, which opens many doors to all possibilities in this world.

I'm so proud to be part of my family, had it not been for the realisation, hard work and dedication starting with mum and dad together with my brothers, sisters, nieces and nephews we would not have achieved our individual successes and talents that each and every one of us holds. I'm proud of you all!

I hope my grandchildren grow to be as ambitious and make their dreams a reality.

I thank Mum for her wise words, wisdom, and gift of cake decorating, all of which I've used to improve my life.

And I'm thankful for Dad's ability to be resourceful which has certainly rubbed off on me.

I thank Marie for being close by at the beginning of my journey in life, especially in the convent.

To Eric, although we don't say it very often, I appreciate you for taking on the task of trying to keep order during our teens, it must have been frustrating at a young age, but it hasn't all gone to waste, as I was inspired by your determination for a better future.

There are so many people I admire in this life, but I'd like to give special thanks to my daughter Arlena, who gave me the best gift ever by teaching me how to use a computer and a mobile phone, and how to navigate the internet. I would have never been in a position to achieve my many goals in later life - this book being one of them. Sorry if I was a pain when trying to take it all in, but I admire your perseverance.

To my wonderful son-in-law Cameron, had it not been your interest in our family's history and background which inspired me to put pen to paper during lockdown, together with your creativity in helping put it together.

Along with all my friends a special thank you to my closest and dearest sister Jacqueline who has always been at my side throughout my highs and lows - love ya!! sis xx

Knowledge is power. Information is liberating. Education is the premise of progress in every society, in every family.

**Kofi Annan**